IN FOC
W9-DDD-464

EASTERN CARIBBEAN

A Guide to the People, Politics and Culture

James Ferguson

LATIN AMERICA BUREAU

INTERLINK BOOKS
NEW YORK

© 1997 James Ferguson. All rights reserved.
First published in 1997

In the U.S.:

Interlink Books
An imprint of Interlink Publishing Group, Inc.
99 Seventh Avenue, Brooklyn, New York 11215

Library of Congress Cataloging-in-Publication Data

Ferguson, James
    Eastern Caribbean in focus: a guide to the people, politics and
    culture /by James Ferguson
        p. cm. (In focus)
    Includes bibliographical references and index.
    ISBN 1-56656-263-5 (pbk)
    1. Antilles, Lesser - Guidebooks. 2. Antilles, Lesser - Description
    and travel I. Title   II. Series: In focus (New York, N.Y.)
    F2001.F42   1997
    917.2904'52-dc21   97-9943
                                                           CIP

In the U.K.:

Latin America Bureau (Research and Action) Ltd,
1 Amwell Street, London EC1R 1UL

The Latin America Bureau is an independent research and publishing
organization. It works to broaden public understanding of issues of
human rights and social and economic justice in Latin America and the
Caribbean.

A CIP catalogue record for this book is available from the British Library
ISBN: 1 899365 09 5

Editing: Duncan Green
Cover photograph: Philip Wolmuth/PANOS Pictures
Cover design: Andy Dark
Design: Liz Morrell
Cartography and diagrams: Kees Prins and Marius Rieff

Already published in the *In Focus* series:
Argentina, Bolivia, Brazil, Colombia, Cuba, Ecuador, Jamaica, Mexico,
Venezuela

Printed and bound in Korea

CONTENTS

INTRODUCTION

Nature is all-powerful in the Eastern Caribbean and human life can seem precarious in its shadow. In her novel *Between Two Worlds*, Simone Schwarz-Bart writes of her native Guadeloupe as a forsaken island, which "arose out of the sea quite recently":

> And rumor has it that it may go as it came, suddenly sink without warning, taking with it its mountains and little sulphur volcano, its green hills where ramshackle huts perch as if hung in the void, and its thousand rivers, so sunny and capricious that the original inhabitants called it the Isle of Lovely Streams.

This sense of beauty and vulnerability has been heightened by recent natural disasters. The hurricanes of 1995 were among the worst in living memory and devastated homes and crops across the region. Tiny Montserrat had barely recovered from the havoc of Hurricane Hugo in 1989 when its long dormant volcano began to show ominous signs of imminent eruption in late 1995 and throughout 1996. As islanders were evacuated, people watched anxiously from neighboring islands, fearing a cataclysm.

Alongside natural catastrophes loom equally menacing economic disasters. The region has always suffered from "boom and bust" commodity cycles; its exports have all too often been vulnerable to volatile markets. Sugar is now a bankrupt museum-piece in most places. The crop which took its place, bananas, is also living on borrowed time, reliant on special trading agreements which will soon end. When the banana industry finally succumbs to market competition, the traditional rural economy of several islands will be ruined.

This leaves only tourism, the final hope of almost all the islands and increasingly their only option. Tourism is a mixed blessing, bringing jobs and money but much else besides. Its impact on Caribbean cultures and societies has yet to be fully understood, but there are many who doubt its long-term benefits.

This guide looks at the thirteen territories which make up the Windward and Leeward Islands as well as Barbados and Trinidad & Tobago. It covers English-, French- and Dutch-speaking islands, independent states, colonies and distant outposts of Europe. It aims to explore the diversity of the islands as well as what they have in common. For within a region of extraordinary variety there is a pattern of shared experience and anticipation: a turbulent history, a vibrant cultural present, and a future as unsettled as next year's hurricane season.

1 ISLANDS AND PEOPLE: THE CARIBBEAN CRUCIBLE

The islands of the Eastern Caribbean come as close to the eternal fantasy of an earthly paradise as almost anywhere in the world. Dramatic forest-clad mountains loom over lush, fertile valleys where, it seems, anything grows. Long white beaches are framed by rows of coconut palms and by a sea which covers the spectrum of shades, from pale aquamarine to deep blue. Cool trade winds temper the tropical heat; rain rarely lasts long.

The topography varies from island to island. Some are spectacularly rugged and mountainous, where steep hillsides are cut by ravines and waterfalls in a dramatic testimony to volcanic activity. Others are more flat and tranquil, sugar-cane and pasture stretching away over a gently undulating landscape. Some are humid and covered with extensive rainforest; others are arid and rely on imported water.

The island arc is geologically quite recent, having been formed between one and two million years ago. Many of the islands are volcanic, with imposing conical mountains and headlands created by lava flows moving down into the sea. Small valleys have been carved out by rivers and streams running down precipitous slopes. In islands such as Martinique, St. Lucia, Dominica and St. Vincent, rainfall is heavy, there are still areas of impenetrable rainforest, and much land cannot be farmed.

Running to the east or Atlantic side of the volcanic chain is another arc of islands, made up primarily of coral limestone. This platform, known as the "foreland," runs the length of the Caribbean and starts from the Bahamas. It meets the Eastern Caribbean in Anguilla and continues via Antigua down to Guadeloupe's easterly Grande-Terre and Barbados. On these islands the landscape is flat and better for plantation agriculture. But water supply is a problem, especially as lower rainfall tends to drain quickly through the permeable limestone rock, running into underground streams.

The islands are commonly divided into two groups, the Leewards and the Windwards. It is unclear how the division came about and several islands have at different times been included in both. The terms leeward and windward refer to the position of the islands in relation to the prevailing easterly wind, the more northerly group, from Anguilla down to Montserrat, being said to lie to the leeward of Barbados or of ships arriving from Europe. The Windwards, on the other hand, stretching from Dominica down to Grenada, lie in the direction from which the prevailing wind blows.

The geography of the Eastern Caribbean has largely determined its history. The first European settlers saw the islands primarily as places in which to grow crops such as sugar-cane for export. Although the flatter terrain of islands such as Barbados and Antigua was more suitable for plantation agriculture, almost every island, even the most mountainous, was used to produce tropical commodities. In the course of its history, the Eastern Caribbean has seen the cultivation of sugar, indigo, cotton, cocoa, tobacco, citrus, and, most recently, bananas.

Some of these crops were introduced into the region from outside and have fundamentally transformed the landscape. Sugar-cane was first cultivated in the Atlantic islands of São Tomé, Madeira, and the Canaries and was introduced into the Caribbean by Spanish colonists. It spread inexorably across the Americas, and only a handful of islands, either too small or too infertile, were spared the plantation system. Citrus fruit and bananas arrived via Asia and Europe and were found to flourish in the tropical climate. Perhaps the most celebrated transplant was that of the breadfruit, brought from the South Pacific by Captain Bligh as a source of cheap carbohydrate for slaves. After the mutiny aboard the notorious *Bounty*, his second expedition in 1793 was more successful, and cuttings from the first breadfruit tree in the Caribbean can still be seen in St. Vincent's Botanic Gardens.

More recently, the islands' scenery and climate have been their chief assets in attracting tourists from North America and Europe. Tourism is now by far the biggest industry in the Eastern Caribbean, and every island depends on the daily arrival of jetloads of visitors for income and employment. Some, such as Barbados, are mass market destinations; others, like Dominica or St. Vincent, receive far fewer visitors because they lack extensive tourist amenities and airports capable of handling large jets. There are exclusive enclaves, like Mustique, which cater to a millionaire clientele and "down-market" package destinations.

Hurricanes and Volcanoes

The benign climatic conditions which draw hundreds of thousands of visitors to the islands have another, more unpredictable, aspect. Hurricanes are the scourge of the Eastern Caribbean, and every year between July and November the region is on more or less permanent alert for signs of impending storms which rise in the Atlantic and move northwest, sometimes extending as far as 500 miles in width. These can create wind speeds of almost 125 miles per hour with bursts of 180 miles per hour or more. A passing hurricane can be devastating, ripping roofs off houses, blowing cars over, and washing boats out of the sea and smashing them. When Hurricane Hugo carved a swathe through Montserrat in 1989, it wrecked 95 per cent of the island's houses and caused $260 million of damage.

There is concern that hurricanes are becoming more frequent, perhaps as a result of global warming or other climatic change. In 1995 a series of

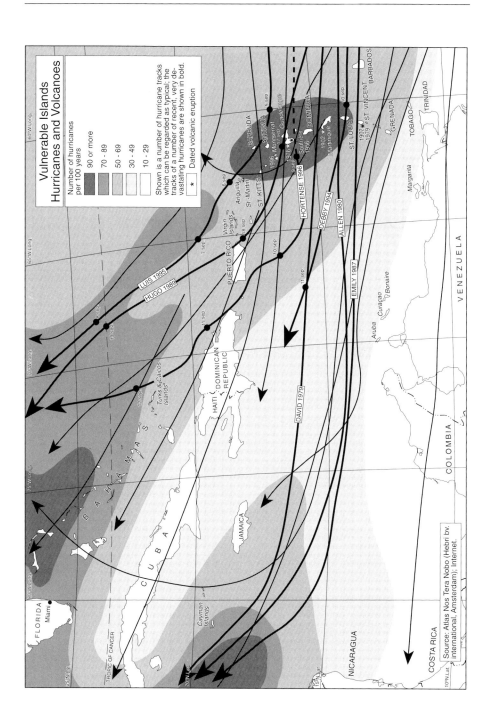

Vulnerable Islands
Hurricanes and Volcanoes

Number of hurricanes
per 100 years

- 90 or more
- 70 - 89
- 50 - 69
- 30 - 49
- 10 - 29

★ Dated volcanic eruption

Shown is a number of hurricane tracks which can be regarded as typical; the tracks of a number of recent, very devastating hurricanes are shown in bold.

LUIS 1995
HUGO 1989
HORTENSE 1996
DEBBY 1994
ALLEN 1980
EMILY 1987
DAVID 1979

FLORIDA
Miami
TROPIC OF CANCER

B A H A M A S

C U B A

Cayman Islands

JAMAICA

HAITI
DOMINICAN REPUBLIC

Turks & Caicos Islands*

PUERTO RICO
Virgin Islands

Anguilla
St-Martin
ST. KITTS

BARBUDA
ANTIGUA
1996 Montserrat
1996 Guadeloupe
Souffrière 1996
DOMINICA
1902 ★ Martinique
ST. LUCIA
1902 ★
1979 ★ ST. VINCENT
BARBADOS

GRENADA
TOBAGO
TRINIDAD

Margarita
Aruba Curaçao Bonaire

NICARAGUA

COSTA RICA

COLOMBIA

VENEZUELA

Source: Atlas Nos Tera Nobo (Hebri bv. international, Amsterdam); Internet.

storms and hurricanes, of which the worst was Hurricane Luis, which cut through Anguilla, Antigua and Guadeloupe. Fortunately, warning systems and civil defense procedures have improved significantly, and loss of life is much smaller than it used to be. Most islands now have hurricane shelters in sturdy buildings such as churches and community centers.

Situated where Atlantic and Caribbean tectonic plates meet, the chain of islands from Saba down to Grenada sit on top of the boiling magma which bubbles up between the plates. The resulting upward pressure is the force behind the volcanic eruptions which have punctuated the region's history. There are still active volcanoes on Montserrat, Guadeloupe, Martinique and St. Vincent, and in St. Lucia and Dominica "fumaroles" produce regular emissions of steam which relieve the pressure below ground. *Soufrière* is the name given to volcanoes throughout the region, derived from the French word for the evil-smelling sulphur which sometimes accompanies the steam.

Imperial Reminders

In the middle of Bridgetown, the bustling capital of Barbados, stands a statue of Horatio Nelson, the British admiral whose exploits against the French are traditionally celebrated in British history books. He looks towards a war memorial commemorating the men of Barbados who fought for Britain in two world wars. Both monuments are in Trafalgar Square, a short walk away from the shops and crowds of Broad Street, and here too is the parliament building, with its stained glass windows depicting English monarchs from James I to Victoria. Out of town, the place names have an English ring; the popular south coast tourist resorts are called Hastings and Worthing; just inland, villages such as Clapham or Highgate evoke suburban London.

Barbados is often known as "Little England". Despite attaining independence from Britain in 1966, the island seems to pride itself on its Englishness. Cricket is played on village greens, Yorkshire pudding appears on hotel menus, and solid Anglican churches, reminiscent of an English village, dot a gently rolling landscape which writers have compared to Dorset or Cornwall. To some extent, the illusion is promoted by the island's tourist board, keen to project an image which appeals to British visitors. Yet, more profoundly, Barbados' "English" identity is also a reflection of almost 350 years of unbroken colonial rule, which began in 1627. Alone among the former British possessions, Barbados never changed hands during centuries of European rivalry in the Caribbean. When Britain declared war against Germany in 1939, the Barbadian politician, Grantley Adams, is reputed to have cabled George VI with the message, "Go on England, Little England is behind you."

160   THE SPHERE   [FEBRUARY 14, 1903

RESTLESS MONT PELÉE: *The Latest Photographs.*

Mont Pelée on January 4, 11.30 a.m.
Taken by a member of a party which landed from the *Argonaut* on January 4. This great mass of dust-laden steam arose while the party were on there

Mont Pelée on January 4, 11.30 a.m.
These photographs show that the volcano was by no means at rest a month ago. The view was taken from the ruins of St. Pierre, looking northward

Mary Evans Picture Library

The Death of Saint Pierre

Unusual activity in Montserrat caused the evacuation of communities living near the Soufrière Hills volcano in 1995 and 1996, while in St. Vincent, La Soufrière erupted on Good Friday 1979 causing extensive agricultural damage but no loss of life.

The worst volcanic disaster in the region's history was the eruption of Mont Pelée in Martinique in May 1902. In the space of minutes, the town of Saint Pierre, then the capital of the French colony and the "Paris of the Antilles," was obliterated, and an estimated 30,000 people were killed in a lethal mix of poisonous gas and red-hot ash. Only one person is known to have survived the eruption, a convicted murderer named Cyparis who was being held in an underground prison cell. He was pardoned shortly afterwards and spent the rest of his life as an exhibit in a traveling Barnum & Bailey circus.

Ironically, the death toll at Saint Pierre could easily have been averted, as the authorities had ample warning of an impending eruption. Several smaller explosions preceded the final blast, and there were many reports of strange phenomena such as boiling rivers and fleeing wildlife. But an election was imminent and the Governor sought to allay fears and urged the town's inhabitants not to abandon their homes.

Today, there is still a town called Saint Pierre, rebuilt on the site of what was considered the most sophisticated and sinful place in the Caribbean. It is smaller than the "Petit Paris" of the nineteenth century. Newer houses and shops stand among the ruins of what were formerly large warehouses and the homes of prosperous merchants. A museum contains ghoulish exhibits – plates and glasses fused into strange shapes, a church bell melted like plasticine – while scientists continually monitor Mont Pelée for further warning signs.

Not all Barbadians like to see themselves as "Little Englanders." Intellectuals and artists such as the poet Kamau Brathwaite stress the African ancestry of the majority of Barbadians and the experience of slavery and exploitation. While the "heritage" industry portrays Barbados as a tropical outpost of Britain, historians place more emphasis on the legacy of forced labour and the plantation economy which has forged the island's modern identity.

France in the Caribbean

Some 125 miles northwest of Barbados lies a department of France – Martinique. Neither a colony nor a dependency, Martinique is an integral part of the French Republic, on an equal footing with any department in Normandy or Provence. To arrive there after staying in any English-speaking island is to experience genuine culture shock. Richer, more developed, more consumerist, Martinique is full of French hypermarkets, French cars, and French tourists. Its capital, Fort-de-France, is clogged with lines of Peugeots and Renaults, while the suburban supermarkets are stocked with Camembert and champagne. The island's Frenchness is even more tangible than Barbadian Englishness; in terms of consumption, culture, and aspirations, most Martinicans look across the Atlantic to the *métropole*.

The relative luxury of many Martinicans' lifestyle is the result of billions of francs of French subsidy. Neither Martinique, Guadeloupe nor Guyane (the three so-called *départements d'outre-mer* in the Caribbean region) produce enough wealth to support such a First World standard of living. Instead, France pays the salaries of legions of civil servants and transfers funding in many other ways, creating an artificial economy and, some argue, a dependency syndrome.

Few Martinicans talk of independence from France and even fewer would vote for it. The island's status as a department ensures its continuing prosperity at the expense of a clear-cut identity. But if most agree that severing links with France would spell economic disaster, some Martinicans dislike what they see as French cultural imperialism. Central authority rests in Paris (despite recent moves towards "regionalization"), provoking resentment against bureaucracy and the imposition of alien values. There is a movement to defend the Creole spoken by all Martinicans against the official French of government and legal officialdom. There is also a growing interest in improved links with neighboring Caribbean countries.

The Dutch Islands

A further 250 miles north, a precipitous volcanic outcrop rises steeply out of the Caribbean sea. The island of Saba, with its population of 1,100, has no beaches, no tourist resorts, and had to wait until 1963 for its alarmingly short airfield to be built on its only piece of flat terrain. This remote and unspoilt place, along with nearby Sint Eustatius and Sint Maarten and more distant Bonaire and Curaçao, is part of the Netherlands Antilles and, as such, part of the Kingdom of the Netherlands. The head of state is Queen Beatrix, the currency is the local version of the guilder, and Dutch is the official language.

But although Saba has pretty, white-painted, wooden houses with green shutters and neat gardens, its connections with the Netherlands are more constitutional than cultural. All Sabans speak English and most have English names such as Johnson or Hassell, being for the most part descendants of English and Scottish settlers. The Dutch flag flies over government offices in the tiny capital, The Bottom, but the presence of the Dutch state is mostly imperceptible. Even though Sabans are meant to learn Dutch at school, few carry on with it, and television is beamed in from the U.S. In this distant corner of the Dutch Kingdom, it is hard to fathom what advantage the government in The Hague receives from underwriting Saba's budget at the cost of $500 per inhabitant every year.

Throughout the Eastern Caribbean the presence and legacy of Europe take many different forms. The British, French, and Dutch governments still administer dependencies or departments in more than ten separate territories. Others such as Antigua, Dominica, and St. Kitts only became independent from Britain in the 1970s and 1980s. Many of the older generation grew up within the British Empire.

But Europe's is but one of the varied influences in an extraordinarily diverse and fragmented region. Increasingly, the small societies of the Eastern Caribbean are exposed to a range of North American contacts in the shape of tourists, consumer goods, and media. Almost every island receives U.S. satellite television, and news about Washington is much more easily available than that from neighboring islands. American music, fashions, and fast food have a foothold in all the region's societies. At the same time, people from the Eastern Caribbean have traditionally viewed the U.S. as a land of opportunity, and many have settled there.

Arawaks and Caribs

Caribbean history did not begin in 1492 with the arrival of Christopher Columbus. By the time the Genoese explorer and his expedition came across the islands, a long process of migration and conflict had already taken place. The first inhabitants of the Eastern Caribbean are now known as the Arawaks, and they probably moved from the mainland of South America to Trinidad and up the island chain somewhere between 4000 and 500 BC. They lived in tribal communities, village-based and ruled by a chieftain or *cacique*, and were accomplished boat-builders and fishermen. Archaeological discoveries have also revealed developed skills in pottery and woodwork as well as elaborate religious carvings. Words such as hammock, tobacco, and hurricane are derived from their languages.

The Arawaks were in turn pursued by the Caribs, who gave their name to the region. They also moved northwards through the islands, travelling by canoe. Hostile and well-organized, they easily killed or drove away the Arawaks in raids on their settlements. The Caribs practiced polygamy and incorporated many captured Arawak women into their communities. The women, for the most part, tended the fields, while the men were adept at fishing as well as warfare.

When Columbus arrived in the Caribbean, he was at first hospitably received by the Arawaks in larger islands such as Hispaniola (today Haiti and the Dominican Republic) and Cuba. The Caribs, however, violently resisted any attempt by Europeans to establish settlements and carried out some devastating attacks. As a result, Carib communities survived in some of the smaller islands much longer than the more peaceful Arawaks, who were nearly all killed by hunger, disease or violence within 50 years of Columbus' first landing. In Dominica and St. Vincent, in particular, the Caribs fended off European colonization until well into the eighteenth century. Their ferocity won them grudging respect, but they were also demonized by European travellers who painted them as cannibals. Eventually, nearly all died out, often in a spirit of defiance. In Grenada the last Caribs leaped from a cliff on the north coast in mass suicide rather than be captured by the French.

The last "pure" Caribs today number no more than a hundred. They still live on the rugged east coast of Dominica on a territory granted to them by the British in 1903. Most families in the village of Salybia and the surrounding settlements are of mixed Carib-African descent, but a few claim to be the direct descendants of the much-feared people who fought off Spanish, French, and English expeditions. They still make a living from boatbuilding and fishing, but selling crafts to tourists now provides an alternative livelihood.

In neighboring St. Vincent a few hundred people are believed to be the descendants of Caribs and the so-called "black Caribs" – a mix of indigenous people and escaped African slaves. So hostile were the black Caribs to British colonial rule that in 1796 the authorities rounded them up after a series of battles and deported them *en masse* to the island of Roatán off the coast of Honduras, leaving only a few scattered families behind.

European Settlers

Although Columbus was the first European to arrive in the Caribbean and gave names to many of its islands, he was not greatly interested in the smaller territories of the Eastern Caribbean. Spanish settlement was limited, and with the exception of Trinidad, Spain made little effort to establish colonies.

By the mid-seventeenth century, it was the British, French, and, to a lesser extent, Dutch, who were the main colonizing powers.

The Europeans who came to live and work in the Caribbean colonies were a mixture of social classes and aspirations. Some, already wealthy, saw the plantation economy as a quick route to further riches and formed the nucleus of a landed gentry or "plantocracy." Others, less rich, hoped to make a quick fortune in a society less rigidly hierarchical than that at home. There were also the poor, attracted by the promise of work, food, and perhaps eventually their own piece of land. Inevitably, the prospect of a new life also drew some of society's less salubrious elements towards the Caribbean. Some of them joined the ranks of the buccaneers who preyed on merchant ships. What emerged was a picaresque mix of would-be aristocrats and paupers, artisans and thieves, priests and mercenaries.

From the outset, the colonial authorities were hampered by labor shortages. The indigenous population was either quickly wiped out or too hostile to use as a workforce. African slaves were at first too expensive and their supply unreliable, so colonies such as Barbados and St. Kitts encouraged laborers from Europe to come and work in the fields. Some came as indentured laborers, working for an agreed period of time in return for subsistence and the promise of some land. Others had less choice and were sent in chains as common criminals or political deportees.

Since the seventeenth century Barbados has had a small "poor white" population, some descended from the prisoners transported in 1686 in the wake of the failed Monmouth rebellion against James II. Today, there are still poor white communities in the eastern parish of St. John, some of which have refused to intermarry with the majority black population. Similar groups exist in Grenada, Guadeloupe and some of the smaller French islands such as Saint-Barthélémy, where descendants of Breton fishermen still outnumber black islanders.

The lives of the poor whites, as recorded by priests and other contemporary observers, were hard and often short. Overworked in disease-ridden tropical conditions, many succumbed quickly to exhaustion and died. Those who survived wanted their own land and left the plantation as soon as they could. As a result, there was never enough labor for the ever-spreading cane fields. The sugar islands were soon to become slave islands.

Out of Africa

Today's population of the Eastern Caribbean is overwhelmingly descended from the hundreds of thousands of Africans who were brought over as slaves in the course of three centuries. The abolition of slavery was decreed in the British colonies in 1833, in the French territories in 1848, and in the Dutch Caribbean in 1863, but its legacy persists in many different ways. Attitudes towards agricultural work, race relations, and perceptions of individual and community identity are all deeply marked by the historic experience of slavery.

Of the twelve million African slaves who made the crossing to the plantations of the Americas, only a relatively small number came to the Eastern Caribbean. Compared to the huge slave systems of Brazil, the U.S. and islands such as Cuba and Hispaniola, the smaller islands of the region were relatively insignificant. When, at abolition, planters in the British colonies submitted lists of slaves in order to claim compensation from the government in London, the numbers ranged from 5,026 (Montserrat) and 7,225 (Nevis) to 23,500 (Antigua) and 66,638 (Barbados). In contrast, Jamaica's planters claimed 255,290 slaves, while there were estimated to be 500,000 in Hispaniola at the time of the 1791 slave revolution.

But slavery was nevertheless almost universal, and even those islands unsuited to large-scale sugar cultivation imported slaves from Africa. Some, such as Dutch Sint Eustatius, specialized as entrepôts, re-exporting slaves to other islands. Others used slaves as domestic servants or artisans.

African slavery in the Caribbean began in 1501 when the Spanish King authorized the Governor of Hispaniola to import black slaves from Spain. At first, Spanish and Portuguese slavers competed for the lucrative business, trying to claim monopolies and royal protection. But by the seventeenth century, they had been joined by slave-traders from Britain, France, Holland, Sweden, and Denmark in an international free-for-all.

The islands imported thousands of slaves each year simply to replace those who died or escaped. In the course of the seventeenth century, Barbados averaged some 3,100 new arrivals each year, while Antigua and St. Kitts both received over 1,000 annually. Mortality rates were appalling, and in some islands slave-traders struggled to keep up, as more slaves died than they could replace with new shiploads. In Antigua, planters openly debated the advantages of working their slaves to death against the cost of replacing them.

Even before the slaves landed, the journey from Africa, known as the Middle Passage, also took a grim toll. The Trinidadian historian Eric Williams has estimated that three out of ten slaves died on the ships which brought them to the Caribbean. Overcrowding, disease and sheer despair meant that millions never arrived. Those who did could expect to be parted from family and community in the terrifying process of selection which took place in the region's slave markets. There followed a brutal regime of hard labor, poor food, and routine punishment, meted out by overseers often drawn from the ranks of the poor whites.

Slavery transformed the region's demography, turning the islands' populations into small white minorities and large black majorities. In Grenada, for instance, there were two black slaves for every white in 1700; by

Slaves at work in a sugar mill   *Mary Evans Picture Library*

1783 the ratio was 25 to one. This equation enabled the sugar plantations to reach their export targets, but also filled the planters with daily dread of insurrection.

Uprisings occurred frequently (see Chapter Two), but slave resistance also took other forms. Many fled the plantations to join rebel groups in the mountains. Known as "Maroons," these bands formed communities based on African social structures and often evaded the attacks of the islands' militias, posing a threat of their own to the plantations. Other slaves managed to poison their masters or their servants and animals, while "passive resistance" in the form of deliberate sloth and incompetence was commonplace.

Most importantly, the slaves preserved their cultural identities despite the cruelty and debasement of plantation life. Language, music, religious faith, and a host of customs survived what the planters hoped would be a process of deculturation. These cultural expressions evolved and were modified by other influences – from other parts of Africa, from other migrant groups, from the planters' own ideology – to form the basis of a unique Creole, or Caribbean, culture.

From the outset of slavery, white men abused and exploited black women. Out of these unequal and largely coercive relationships were born children of mixed parentage, known as "mulattoes," "coloreds" or *gens de couleur*. At first a small minority, they came to represent a distinct class in colonial and post-colonial society, with its own identity and interests. Often rejected by the white elite and hostile to the black majority, the colored middle stratum was to evolve into the commercial and administrative class of every island.

Indian Migration

The abolition of slavery created another labor shortage, and the planters and colonial authorities turned to fresh sources of workers. Migrants from Africa, Madeira, and China were encouraged to come as indentured laborers, but by far the largest group to fill the labour gap were the half-million indentured workers from India who arrived in the Caribbean. In the Eastern Caribbean, their preferred destination was Trinidad, which received 145,000 between 1838 and 1917. Smaller, but significant, numbers went to Guadeloupe, Martinique, St. Lucia and Grenada.

Indo-Trinidad

In what is probably one of the most cosmopolitan cultures in the world, India is an ever-present influence in modern Trinidad. In rural areas, dhoti-clad farmers work the rice fields, while water buffalo graze amidst huge expanses of coconut palms. Hindu prayer flags stand outside homes, and villages contain as many Muslim mosques and Hindu temples as churches. In districts of Port of Spain, the streets are lined with Indian-owned bazaars, whose blaring music competes with the calypso, soca or reggae blasting out from passing buses.

Approximately 40 per cent of Trinidadians are of Indian descent, making up the island's largest ethnic group. A mix of mostly rural Hindus, urban Muslims, and some Christians, they are the driving force in agriculture and commerce.

For many years, black Trinidadians regarded Indians with disdain, disparaging them as "coolies" who came to provide cheap labor in the wake of abolition. Racial tension was commonplace and Indians were generally the poorest sector of Trinidadian society. The People's National Movement (PNM) which dominated the island's politics after its first election victory in 1956 was generally considered black nationalist, and few Indians supported it. In the first 30 years after independence Indians were marginalized.

But in 1986 widespread disillusionment with the PNM allowed a coalition of smaller parties to win power, and Basdeo Panday, an Indian-descended trade unionist, became Deputy Prime Minister. The coalition subsequently broke up, and Panday formed his own United National Congress. Then, in November 1995, Panday made history by winning enough seats in an election to become Trinidad's first Indian Prime Minister. For the first time, Trinidadian Indians had turned their numerical majority into political power.

Today's island societies have evolved from a complex combination of peoples and cultural influences. Each is different and unique, with its own mix of historical and ethnic ingredients. Martinique, for instance, with its still powerful white elite of so-called *békés*, is different from poorer, darker Guadeloupe, where large-scale Indian immigration took place. Barbados, which has a significant white upper class, is socially distinct from St. Lucia or Dominica, in which small farmers of African descent are a powerful political group. Just as landscape varies from island to island, so does the imprint of an often eventful history.

2   HISTORY AND POLITICS: LOST EMPIRES

Brimstone Fortress on the east coast of St. Kitts is a forbidding symbol of military might. Hewn out of volcanic rock, its massive walls were intended to protect its British garrison against attack by the French. In its heyday it could house 1,000 troops, with their own parade ground, kitchens, and hospital. Its cannons point menacingly out to sea and, more disconcertingly, inland towards the green slopes of Mount Liamuiga and some invisible adversary.

Dating from 1690 and restored in the 1980s, Brimstone Fortress is one of many citadels and forts which litter the Eastern Caribbean. On a clear day, a visitor can look over a spectacular panorama of sea and make out the islands of Sint Eustatius and Saba (Dutch), St. Barthélémy and St. Martin (French), and Montserrat (British). The proximity of the European neighbors explains the magnitude of Brimstone's defenses. There was also the bitter experience of 1782 when 8,000 French laid siege for a month and eventually captured the fort, prompting the British to build still more defenses after ejecting their adversaries the following year.

Looking down from what was called "the Gibraltar of the West Indies" (it too has tame apes), one also sees the neat shapes of sugar-cane fields stretching down towards the sea. Nowadays, St. Kitts' sugar industry is in semi-permanent crisis, kept afloat only by low wages and preferential export access into Europe. But in the seventeenth century, the crop was worth fighting for, and the small and seemingly insignificant islands of the region were the object of superpower rivalry.

Cockpit of Europe

The Spanish were the first European nation to establish colonies in the Caribbean, but founded few lasting settlements beyond the large islands of Cuba, Hispaniola, Puerto Rico, and Jamaica. They were dislodged from Trinidad by the British in 1797 and abandoned claims to other Eastern Caribbean islands without a fight.

The real competition was between the British, the French, and to a lesser extent the Dutch, with Sweden and Denmark playing minor parts in the colonial free-for-all. Their race for Caribbean supremacy started in St. Kitts in 1623, when an expedition led by Sir Thomas Warner claimed the island for Britain. It was swiftly followed by Pierre Belain d'Esnambuc's rival French expedition. The two groups of settlers had a common enemy in the indigenous Caribs and agreed to share the island, an agreement which lasted, albeit with regular disputes, until 1713. Together the British and French wiped out the Caribs in a massacre at Bloody Point in 1626.

St. Kitts was the launch pad for both British and French expansion. The British claimed islands like Montserrat and Antigua, and the French settled on Martinique and Guadeloupe. Other islands were impossible to colonize because of indigenous resistance, and both nations had their expeditions driven away. But in many territories a state of almost permanent war between Britain and France prevailed for almost two centuries, with invasions and counter-invasions transferring sovereignty with dizzying frequency.

Only Barbados experienced unbroken rule, by Britain, throughout the entire colonial period. Other islands changed hands with every new naval expedition dispatched from Bristol or Nantes. Tobago came under different rule no fewer than 29 times until 1802, when Britain established lasting control. Sint Eustatius changed flag on 22 occasions before the Dutch claimed uncontested sovereignty. St. Lucia underwent fourteen invasions and counter-invasions before Britain staked a permanent claim.

A succession of treaties (rarely honored for long) marked the European powers' attempts to outdo their rivals in the division of the Caribbean. In 1763, for instance, when Britain and France signed a peace treaty, London had to decide whether to return Guadeloupe or Canada (both of which had been captured during the war). The fact that Britain opted to keep Canada was greeted with jubilation by the French who much preferred their Caribbean island to what Voltaire dismissed as "a few acres of snow." The treaties of Paris (1763), Versailles (1783), and Paris (1814) formalized transfers of sovereignty, but these were soon overtaken by further disputes and battles.

The fighting was often motivated by military concerns, as in the case of Tobago, which was viewed as an ideal base for expeditions into the South American mainland. The Eastern Caribbean was also prized as the first point of arrival for most ships crossing the Atlantic from Europe. Fortresses sprang up throughout the islands, and the European powers built naval bases such as Nelson's Dockyard in Antigua.

Another consideration was trade, and the rival powers often raided one another's ports and warehouses. Sometimes issues of sovereignty became indistinguishable from mere piracy. During the American War of Independence, Dutch Sint Eustatius was an important source of supplies for the American rebels, a situation deplored by the British. When in 1776 the Dutch authorities fired a cannon in recognition of a ship flying the colors of the independent United States of America, the British found a pretext for spectacular revenge. Five years later, a British fleet entered the port, confiscated all the ships and goods it found and sailed away back across the Atlantic.

But the real reason for the intense rivalry of the eighteenth century was the profitability of "King Sugar". "The profits of a sugar plantation," wrote

Sir Walter Raleigh victorious over the Spanish in Trinidad

Mary Evans Picture Library

the economist Adam Smith in 1776, "are generally much greater than those of any other cultivation that is known either in Europe or America." Although relatively small and technologically backward, the plantations of the Eastern Caribbean produced thousands of tons of sugar each year, enriching both the planters and the metropolitan governments which took their share of duties and taxes.

Not that the planters and the far-away authorities in London or Paris saw eye to eye. The Caribbean landowners resented being forced to sell their commodities to a single buyer back in the "mother country," while the metropolitan governments often viewed the planters as inefficient and disloyal. Conflicts of interest were endemic to their relationship. The sugar-producers of a British island, for example, would inevitably oppose the capture of a French island since it would put more sugar on the market in London and lower their prices. Conversely, the European governments resolutely blocked any move towards free trade on the part of their colonies.

Inter-European conflict reached a peak in the 1780s. In 1781 and 1782 the French recaptured Sint Eustatius, Tobago, St. Kitts, Nevis, and Montserrat. Under its commander, de Grasse, the French fleet seemed to have decisively defeated the British. But in 1782 a reformed British fleet, commanded by Admiral George Rodney, attacked the French ships near Les Saintes, between Dominica and Guadeloupe. By managing to break de Grasse's formation, Rodney captured seven ships and scattered the rest, winning a battle which turned the balance of military supremacy in Britain's favor. In the ensuing Treaty of Versailles, Britain recovered Grenada, St. Vincent, St. Kitts, Nevis, Montserrat and Dominica.

Political events in Europe sharpened conflict in the Eastern Caribbean still further. The French Revolution of 1789 sent shock waves through the region, terrifying the conservative planters with the specter of insurrection and inspiring the slaves with the promise of liberty. In 1794 the revolutionary Convention in France dispatched a commissioner, Victor Hugues, to Guadeloupe to enforce its law abolishing slavery. His other task was to mobilize the freed slaves as a force with which to harass the British in their neighboring colonies. Acting as an *agent provocateur*, Hugues successfully encouraged revolts in St. Vincent and Grenada. In Grenada, a local mulatto planter of French descent, Julien Fédon, led a slave rebellion in 1795 which lasted fifteen months and threatened to overthrow the colonial authorities. So terrified of the French Revolution were the planters of Martinique that they invited the British to occupy their island between 1794 and 1802 and prevent the abolition of slavery.

The Other War

The almost perpetual upheaval in the region was not only the result of inter-European rivalry. Slavery itself created its own tensions, which periodically erupted into full-scale violence. One of the first revolts took place in the French part of St. Kitts in 1639 when 60 black slaves escaped and built a fort on the peak of Mount Liamuiga. It took 500 troops to put down the uprising, and the leaders were burned alive or quartered. Insurrections or conspiracies followed in Barbados (1649), Guadeloupe (1656), and Barbados (1675 and 1692).

The heyday of the slave revolt was the 18th century. In 1736 a plot was hatched among the slaves of Antigua which nearly brought down the entire colonial edifice. An uprising was planned for October 11, the anniversary of King George II's accession, when the planters were due to hold a ball in the Governor's residence. The conspirators planned to blow up the residence and massacre every white on the island. Only the coincidental death of the Governor's son led to the ball being canceled and the discovery of the plot. The ringleaders were tortured and burned alive.

In the course of the century slaves organized their own forms of resistance and rebellion. Apart from full-scale insurrections in Guadeloupe, Martinique, Nevis, and Montserrat, there were frequent disturbances and acts of sabotage on individual plantations. The culmination of the struggle for self-emancipation took place in 1791 in distant Saint Domingue, the French part of Hispaniola, when hundreds of thousands of slaves began a thirteen-year war against their masters. The impact of the Saint Domingue revolution and the eventual creation of independent Haiti in 1804 was felt throughout the Eastern Caribbean. Slaves in Martinique, like those in Saint Domingue, demanded their freedom; in 1789 a letter, signed "all the Negroes," was sent to the Governor threatening to "set fire to the whole colony and drown it in blood."

As French planters fleeing the Saint Domingue revolution arrived in Trinidad and other islands, fears of similar uprisings mounted. The French revolutionary Convention had abolished slavery in its colonies in 1794 (partly as an attempt to defuse the Saint Domingue civil war), but Napoleon Bonaparte reinstated it in Guadeloupe in 1802. The result was a further series of revolts across the region.

The End of Slavery

Fear of violent self-emancipation was a compelling reason for abolishing slavery altogether. The Governor of Barbados wrote to the British Secretary of State for the Colonies in 1819 that "the public mind is ever tremblingly alive to the dangers of insurrection," and the cost of maintaining large militias to repress such insurrections was prohibitive.

At the same time, a growing humanitarian movement in Europe was vociferous in its condemnation of slavery's abuses. Individuals such as William Wilberforce and Thomas Clarkson formed the Anti-Slavery Society in London and used their influence to sway public and political opinion. In France a group of prominent intellectuals and politicians, led by Victor Schoelcher, also pressed for abolition. Both movements argued that slavery was inhumane, un-Christian, and perhaps most importantly, economically unviable.

It was the economic argument which proved most persuasive. The crucial factor was that sugar production across the region was either static or declining. The small and mostly inefficient plantations of the Eastern Caribbean could not compete on the open market with big producers such as Cuba. Yields were lower, prices were higher, and the overheads associated with maintaining slaves were a large part of the problem. An additional difficulty was the increasing shortage and rising price of slaves. As economic problems beset the sugar islands, they could not afford to import as many goods from Europe, reducing their importance to the metropolitan economies. By the 1820s, the fierce rivalries between the European colonizers had died away.

The gospel of free trade and capitalism was slavery's undoing. The discovery of beet sugar by a Prussian chemist in 1747 meant that Europe would no longer depend on imports of cane sugar from the tropics. An important power group of European beet growers and refiners grew in strength in the nineteenth century, opposed to the Caribbean planters and their supporters. Cheaper to produce and employing European workers, beet sugar seemed more attractive than the over-priced product of the slave plantation. There was also competition from other cane producers in Brazil, India, and other parts of the world.

The interests of European producers, shippers, manufacturers, and consumers finally outweighed those of the plantocracy. It was, in a sense, a

Abolition in the French Caribbean, 1848   *Mary Evans Picture Library*

struggle between the new industrial middle classes and the old landed aristocracy. Reluctantly, the planters began to accept the inevitable, but abolition did not come quickly. First, the slave trade itself was abolished, by Britain in 1807, France in 1817, and Holland in 1818. Despite a continuing illegal trade, the measures slowed the flow of new slaves into the region and made the system even more unviable. Then came a series of reforms involving conditions and the gradual emancipation of certain categories of slaves. When abolition was finally decreed by Britain in 1833, it was stipulated that the former slaves would have to remain the unpaid "apprentices" of their masters for a further seven years – later reduced to four. France decreed immediate abolition in 1848, as did Holland in 1863.

Peasants and Plantations

The end of slavery did not bring ruin and anarchy, as the planters had predicted. A series of draconian laws restricted what the former slaves could do and where they could settle. In the islands where land was scarce, many had no choice but to remain as wage-laborers on the plantations. In other territories, many opted for life as small farmers, settling on marginal land or paying rent to local landowners or the Crown. These peasant communities formed villages, grew crops for local consumption, and cultivated some of the region's new agricultural exports such as nutmeg, cocoa, and cotton.

Some ex-slaves specialized in fishing, and seafaring villages grew up along the more placid Caribbean coastlines.

Abolition also encouraged the emergence of an urban working class, based in port towns such as Saint Pierre, Castries, and Bridgetown. Here there was work in shipping, warehousing, and all the other activities associated with the islands' export trade.

The main export continued to be sugar and production increased steadily until the 1880s, even though its profitability declined. The advent of Indian indentured laborers in Trinidad enabled the planters to export more than 55,000 tons of sugar in 1882 compared to 13,000 in 1828. Some islands, such as Antigua and Barbados, remained completely dependent on sugar for export earnings. Others, like Dominica and St. Vincent, diversified their exports, thanks largely to their small farmers.

The second half of the nineteenth century witnessed the slow decline of the old plantocracy. Many planters simply abandoned their estates and became absentee landowners; huge tracts of prime land lay fallow and neglected. At the same time, the colored or mulatto middle class grew in importance and power, taking an ever-greater stake in the island's businesses and professions. For the great majority of blacks and poor Indians, life did not improve dramatically with the arrival of formal freedom. Wages on the plantation were abysmally low, health and education provision almost nonexistent. The possibility of change had arrived, yet the pace of real progress was very slow.

With changing economic roles came demands for fundamental political reform. The British colonies were essentially run by a London-appointed Governor in conjunction with an elected local council. Only males with certain property qualifications could vote in elections, enabling the white minority to exclude all competition. Gradually, however, the colored sector of society began to press for political rights, while the first associations of smallholders and workers were formed at the turn of the century. The pattern was broadly similar in the Dutch colonies, but in Martinique and Guadeloupe universal male suffrage was reintroduced in 1871 (it had been decreed in 1848 and abolished again in 1851), allowing voters to send deputies to parliament in Paris.

Winds of Change

By the start of the twentieth century the Eastern Caribbean's sugar industry was all but bankrupt, outstripped by Cuba, old-fashioned, and uncompetitive in comparison to European and North American beet production. Exports began to shrink; the Caribbean's share (Cuba excluded) of the world market dwindled. The result was stagnation and poverty across the region, particularly in the most sugar-dependent islands. Many thousands were forced to migrate in search of work. Between 1904 and 1914 people left almost every island of the Eastern Caribbean to work in the construction of the Panama Canal.

The First World War brought some relief to the region, as sugar prices rose five-fold due to the damage done to European beet production. During that period the move towards greater democracy gathered pace, and the first trade unions and political organizations began to appear in the 1920s and 1930s. Some of the emerging political leaders were from the colored middle classes and sought greater representation within the colonial system. Others had their support among the peasantry, plantation laborers, and working class and advocated more radical reforms. The colonial authorities grudgingly introduced piecemeal legislation but stopped well short of universal suffrage.

The 1930s suddenly accelerated the momentum of political change. A wave of riots and unrest between 1934 and 1938 brought the plight of the English-speaking islands more urgently to London's attention. Starting in the canefields of Trinidad and St. Kitts, the troubles spread through St. Vincent, St. Lucia and Barbados as protesters went on strike for higher wages and better conditions. The authorities attempted to arrest or deport leaders such as "Buzz" Butler in Trinidad and Clement Payne in Barbados, and called in British warships to restore order. A royal commission, headed by Lord Moyne, was sent by the British government in 1938-9 to investigate the causes of the unrest. When its report was finally published in 1945, it was a damning indictment of colonial neglect.

"Slums of Empire"

Lord Moyne's 400-page survey of conditions in the British colonies painted a grim picture of widespread poverty, poor education and run-down health services. It expressed disquiet at continuing reliance on a ruined sugar industry and called for real attempts to diversify the islands' economies. Moyne and his committee made a special point of visiting the worst slum areas in each island and were appalled at what they found:

It is no exaggeration to say that in the poorest parts of most towns and in many of the country districts a majority of the houses is largely made of rusty corrugated iron and unsound boarding; quite often the original floor has disappeared and only the earth remains, its surface so trampled that it is impervious to any rain which may penetrate through a leaking roof; sanitation in any form and water supply are unknown in such premises... These decrepit homes, more often than not, are seriously overcrowded, and it is not surprising that some of them are dirty and verminous in spite of the praiseworthy efforts of the inhabitants to keep them clean. In short, every condition that tends to produce disease is here to be found in a serious form. The generally insanitary environment gives rise to malaria, worm infection, and bowel diseases; leaking roofs, rotten flooring, and lack of light encourage the spread of tuberculosis, respiratory diseases, worm infections, jigger lesions, and rat-borne diseases...'

The conflict of the 1930s launched the political careers of a series of local leaders who formed unions and parties. Some such as Robert Bradshaw in St. Kitts, Eric Gairy in Grenada, and Vere Bird in Antigua, were trade union organizers from humble backgrounds. Others, like Grantley Adams in Barbados or Eric Williams in Trinidad, were educated, middle-class professionals. Their politics owed much to the moderate socialism of the British Labour Party and most of them founded their own Labor parties with explicit appeal to the poorer segments of society. Their activities inevitably brought them into conflict with the colonial powers, and men such as Bird and Gairy became folk heroes for daring to challenge the local elites.

Assimilation or Independence?

The end of the Second World War ushered in a period of political ferment. The conflict had worsened conditions in every island, cutting off trade links and investment, and many men from English- and French-speaking islands had fought and died in Europe. The war had affected Martinique and Guadeloupe particularly badly, as Admiral Robert and a French fleet had imposed rule in the name of Vichy France and had been blockaded by the U.S. navy. An air of expectancy followed the declaration of peace, and the election of new and radical governments both in Britain and France promised significant reform. American influence, meanwhile, hitherto relatively limited in the Eastern Caribbean, had grown hugely, especially in islands such as Antigua and Trinidad where the British colonial authorities had allowed the U.S. military to establish bases in return for 50 out-of-date warships. Britain's increasing indifference to its colonies, allowed the U.S.a greater role and it began to invest in more developed economics such as Trinidad's.

In 1946 the people of the two French colonies voted overwhelmingly in favor of becoming full-fledged *départements* of the French Republic. Leaving behind their colonial past, Martinique and Guadeloupe attained the same constitutional status as any metropolitan French *département*. The chief architect of so-called "departmentalization" was Aimé Césaire, the Communist Mayor of Fort de France and later founder of his own Parti Progressiste Martiniquais (PPM). Césaire argued that the islands' development would be best guaranteed through assimilation with France while preserving as much political and cultural autonomy as possible. The colonial Governor was replaced with the Prefect, the symbol of central French gov-

Independence ceremony, Trinidad and Tobago

Hulton Getty

ernment, and an elected Council administered local affairs while deputies and senators represented the islands in Paris.

The Dutch islands also opted for assimilation with their former colonial power. They had been the only part of the Dutch empire not to be invaded during the War, and at that time Queen Wilhelmina had promised them a new constitutional arrangement when hostilities ceased. In 1954 the Charter of the Kingdom of the Netherlands was duly proclaimed by Queen Juliana, granting the same status to the Dutch Antilles (Aruba, Bonaire, Curaçao, Saba, Sint Eustatius, and Sint Maarten) as to Holland itself.

French and Dutch policy created a curious anomaly in the form of St. Martin. The island has been shared since 1648 by the two European nations, divided between French Saint Martin and Dutch Sint Maarten. With departmentalization, the French section became a sub-prefecture of Guadeloupe (and part of France), while Sint Maarten became part of the Dutch Kingdom. Today, visitors can drive from France to an outpost of the Netherlands across an almost nonexistent border without leaving a 34-square mile Caribbean island.

In the English-speaking Eastern Caribbean the solutions envisaged by local politicians and colonial authorities were very different. The new political parties were mostly populist in approach, promising to improve the lot of their supporters. When increased representation and suffrage were granted by London after 1944, they became the dominant forces in local government, winning a series of elections in 1951. But while they envisaged running affairs in their own particular islands, the British had another plan for the Caribbean. Aware that small islands would find independence difficult, if not impossible, the British encouraged the idea of a Federation of the West Indies, which would bring the "large" territories of Jamaica and Trinidad together with the smaller islands into a single, federal and self-governing entity.

The idea was largely popular among the people of the Eastern Caribbean islands since they doubted the viability of individual independence. Some politicians, however, were less eager to give up their status as small-island rulers. After eleven years of deliberations, the Federation of the West Indies finally came into being in 1958. Headquartered in Trinidad, it comprised Antigua & Barbuda, Barbados, Dominica, Grenada, Jamaica, Montserrat, St. Kitts, Nevis & Anguilla, St. Lucia, St. Vincent & the Grenadines and Trinidad & Tobago. The prime minister was Grantley Adams of Barbados, and the islands elected 45 members in proportion to their population.

Yet by 1961 the experiment was over, broken up by inter-island rivalry and Jamaica's suspicions that it was subsidizing the smaller, poorer territories. Jamaica withdrew from the Federation, and Prime Minister Eric Williams of Trinidad memorably remarked "one from ten leaves nought." Subsequent federal arrangements also failed.

The collapse of the Federation was a blow to the British government which wanted to rid itself of its Caribbean colonies. Potentially troublesome and no longer economically attractive, the islands were now seen as a liability, and Britain urged them to opt for independence. Some larger ones became independent soon after, Trinidad & Tobago in 1962, Barbados in 1966. Others followed gradually in the 1970s and 1980s. In some cases, it was clear that the islands were reluctant to sever their ties with London, but in return Britain promised financial aid and membership of the Commonwealth. In this respect, British policy was very different from that of France or the Netherlands, which valued a continuing political relationship with their ex-colonies.

Only in a few cases was Britain unable to end the colonial link. Montserrat rejected independence, as did the British Virgin Islands, the Turks & Caicos Islands, and the Cayman Islands. The most embarrassing débâcle, however, occurred in 1969 when Britain invaded tiny Anguilla after it had seceded from St. Kitts & Nevis.

Bay of Piglets

Anguilla, a 35-square mile island of 10,000 people, is one of the least developed of the region's territories. Flat, dry, and mostly covered in scrub, it was less fought-over than many of its neighbors and remained almost continually under British rule. In 1956 it became part of the three-island colony of St. Kitts-Nevis-Anguilla. As the move towards independence gathered pace, administrators in London anticipated that the three islands would become a single, independent state. The date for independence "in association" with Britain was set for 1967.

But the Anguillans had other ideas. Long suspicious and resentful of St. Kitts' domination of the federation, the islanders complained that they were neglected and deprived of resources by the "imperialists" of St. Kitts. Matters worsened when the fiery Robert Bradshaw, the Chief Minister of St. Kitts, threatened to turn Anguilla into "a desert." In 1967 Anguillans rebelled, shots were fired, Kittitian policemen were rounded up and put to sea, and there was even a small and abortive invasion attempt by a group of Anguillans in St. Kitts. A referendum in Anguilla overwhelmingly rejected the association with St. Kitts and demanded protection from Britain.

After months of tension, the British were finally forced to act, and paratroopers and policemen "invaded" the island in 1969 to a rapturous welcome from the rebel Anguillans. Eight years after the Cuban Bay of Pigs drama, the Anguillan fiasco was derided as Britain's "Bay of Piglets." The police stayed until 1972, and Anguilla won its victory over St. Kitts. The federal solution was abandoned, and Anguilla remains a British Dependent Territory in which a Governor works in association with an Executive Council and House of Assembly.

Revolution and Counter-Revolution

The political systems bequeathed by the European powers began to come under increasing strain in the 1960s and 1970s as a wave of radicalism, partly inspired by the 1959 Cuban Revolution, affected the region. Independence movements, sometimes violent in their tactics, grew in strength in Martinique and Guadeloupe; in 1970 Trinidad was shaken by a "Black Power" rebellion.

In some islands the leaders who had come to prominence in the 1930s were still entrenched in power 30 years later. In Antigua, the Bird family developed an unsavory reputation for corruption, while Robert Bradshaw in St. Kitts was criticized by his opponents as a despot. But perhaps the most controversial figure in the region was Eric Gairy, who dominated Grenada's politics from the 1950s onwards. Forming his own violent militia, the Mongoose Gang, Gairy intimidated his opponents and was censured by the British for alleged "squandermania" or corruption. Independence arrived in 1974, and many Grenadians were worried that the eccentric Gairy, who was obsessed with UFOs, would become a dictator.

British paratroopers in Anguilla, 1969   *Popperfoto*

An armed uprising in 1979 overthrew Gairy's government and brought to power a small left-wing group of young Grenadians known as the New Jewel Movement (NJM). They formed a People's Revolutionary Government (PRG) and introduced a series of reforms favoring the rural poor. For four years, the PRG pursued a policy of cooperation between the state and private sector, receiving considerable aid from Cuba. Although opponents questioned its human rights record, the PRG was widely praised, even by the World Bank, for its imaginative economic program. Yet the Grenadian "revo" was anathema to the U.S. and especially the Reagan administration which viewed it through a Cold War prism as a regional security threat and worked to desabilize it.

In October 1983 the NJM was torn apart by factional in-fighting and the island's charismatic prime minister, Maurice Bishop, was murdered by rivals. As a military coup followed Bishop's assassination, the U.S. decided to intervene, invading the island and dismantling what remained of the revolution. A number of U.S. troops, Cuban construction workers and Grenadian civilians were killed in what Reagan called a "rescue mission," yet some Grenadians welcomed the invasion, appalled at the death of Bishop and the other blood-letting.

The Grenada invasion was a setback to left-wing parties across the region, and many conservative parties won elections in the years that followed. Politicians such as Eugenia Charles in Dominica and James "Son" Mitchell in St. Vincent were outspokenly pro-U.S., hoping to attract aid and investment from a Washington still nervous about instability in its "backyard."

By the mid-1990s that instability had largely failed to materialize. There was another uprising in Trinidad in 1990, led by a fundamentalist Muslim group, but the parliamentary system survived. Elsewhere, the independent nations have held regular and free elections, while anti-French feeling in Martinique and Guadeloupe has been contained through reforms and huge subsidies from Paris. Political transformation has been mostly peaceful, with a younger generation of politicians replacing veterans such as Eugenia Charles and St. Lucia's John Compton. To this extent, the Caribbean is no longer, for the moment at least, the potential political "hot spot" that it was in the 1970s. U.S. Strategists are now more concerned with the destabilization caused by the drug industry and related crime.

The real threat to the small-island states now comes less from political upheaval than from the risk of marginalization in the world economy. As the U.S. becomes increasingly involved in regional trade agreements with North and South American states, Caribbean leaders fear that they will lose access to American markets and U.S. aid. This fear has to some extent re-kindled interest in regional integration, as governments recognize that co-operation offers a better chance of economic survival than separatism.

So far, however, plans to form a federation of Windward Island states (Dominica, Grenada, St. Lucia and St. Vincent) have not borne fruit, and there is uncertainty as to how such a federal arrangement would work. As ever, the domestic concerns of local politicians seem to outweigh a regional perspective, and relatively wealthier islands suspect that they will bear a disproportionate financial burden.

Yet there are more positive signs. Politicians and entrepreneurs in the French islands are increasingly interested in forging closer links with their English-speaking neighbors. There is a regional body, the Organization of Eastern Caribbean States (OECS), founded in 1981 and including the four Windward Islands as well as Antigua, Montserrat and St. Kitts & Nevis, upon which deeper integration could be built. The Eastern Caribbean Central Bank in St. Kitts already issues a common currency in eight separate territories, and an Eastern Caribbean Supreme Court operates from St. Lucia. These sub-regional institutions exist alongside the Caribbean Community (CARICOM) which groups thirteen independent countries across the Caribbean in a free-trade agreement. Although the structures for further integration exist, what is lacking is the political will to take the process further and break down age-old barriers of rivalry and suspicion.

3   ECONOMY: AFTER THE PLANTATION

Several times each day the countryside surrounding Grantley Adams International Airport in Barbados reverberates under the roar of incoming jets. Tourists lounging on the beaches of the south coast see the planes glide in low along the horizon before banking westwards for their final descent. The flights from New York and Miami, from Toronto and Montreal, arrive during the day; those from London, Frankfurt, or Zurich come as night is falling. Suddenly, tourists who hours earlier were shivering in distant northern cities find themselves in the humid darkness of a Caribbean night, surrounded by chirping choruses of unseen tree frogs.

The more prosperous are whisked away to the luxury resorts of Sandy Lane or Glitter Bay, where a high season room can cost $500 or more a day. Fellow guests such as Luciano Pavarotti or Joan Collins may have arrived by Concorde. More economy-minded tourists can stay at any of the myriad guesthouses or apartments in places like Worthing or Oistins, where prices start at $50. Here, the supermarkets, bars and fast food outlets which line the coast road cater to more modest tastes.

Both up-market and down-market tourism are vital to Barbados' economy. Over 440,000 tourists stayed in Barbados in 1995, and another 480,000 arrived for a brief visit on a cruise ship. In recent years, tourism has contributed up to 60 per cent of the island's export income, although recession in the U.S. has affected earnings. In 1994, tourism brought in more than ten times more than sugar – once the mainstay of the economy.

Two hundred and fifty miles up the island chain, the economic profile of Dominica is very different. Here, tourism is still in its infancy, and the tiny airports on either side of the island are unable to receive large jets. The visitors who come to the self-styled "nature isle" are mostly interested in its flora and fauna, making Dominica one of the region's most sought-after eco-tourism destinations. A mere 38,000 tourists came to Dominica in 1995, although that figure is rising fast, and another 86,000 came via cruise ships.

Dominica's economic staple is not yet tourism, but bananas. In this extraordinarily precipitous island bananas grow everywhere, invading roadside verges and clinging onto hillsides. Every available inch of land seems to be given over to the fruit, which thrives in the steamy rainforest environment. Since the 1980s, banana exports have comprised most of Dominica's income, and production rose steadily to more than 55,000 tons in 1993. The late 1980s saw a "banana boom" in Dominica and the other three Windward Islands – Grenada, St. Lucia and St. Vincent – and many small farmers were able to buy the Japanese pick-up trucks which bounce along Dominica's pot-holed roads.

But bananas are a notoriously vulnerable crop. There are several devastating diseases which can destroy entire plantations. A hurricane can smash its way through a banana field within seconds, ruining production for many months. Dominica was badly hit by Hurricane Luis in September 1995 and lost a fifth of its banana earnings that year, driving the economy into recession. There is also the threat posed by international trading conditions. For many years, Dominican bananas enjoyed guaranteed entry into the British market at more or less stable prices. But under the European Union's new import regime, Caribbean bananas face increasing competition from cheaper fruit produced in Latin America. Prices received by growers have dropped sharply in recent years, and there are well-founded fears that the EU intends to scrap all preferential treatment for Caribbean bananas before the end of the century.

Tourism and bananas have been the mainstay of Eastern Caribbean economies for the last 40 years. Almost every island in the region relies on tourism for a significant part of its income, while the Windwards along with Martinique and Guadeloupe are highly dependent on banana exports. There are, it seems, few alternatives. The islands are too small to support anything but basic manufacturing for domestic consumption. Their labor costs are not as cheap as those of Haiti or the Dominican Republic, and foreign companies see few advantages in setting up factories so far away from the U.S. or Europe. With the exception of Trinidad, which has oil and gas, the islands have few natural resources.

Throughout their history the islands have exported commodities to the industrialized world and imported manufactured goods in return. They have always produced what they do not consume and consumed what they do not produce. This has created highly "open" economies, vulnerable to commodity price drops and to unequal terms of trade.

King Sugar

Sugar has been both the driving force and the burden of Caribbean economies. Once the proverbial "white gold" of the colonial system, it became the single most tenacious obstacle to development and diversification. For a century after the abolition of slavery, sugar continued to dominate many of the small-island economies, despite falling prices and a declining share of the world market. Even today, thousands of acres throughout the islands are covered by sugar-cane, which usually occupies flat and fertile valley terrain. The sugar industry may have withered away in places like Antigua and St. Vincent, but it remains an important, if seemingly

Kitts & Nevis

St. Eustatius

Saba

Antigua & Barbuda

Traces of the old colonial powers are to be found in the buildings and streets of every Eastern Caribbean town. Despite the advent of concrete blocks and corrugated iron, the region's capitals still reflect the tastes and styles of the former "motherlands" – Britain, France, and the Netherlands. The tourism industry has helped to preserve some of this architecture, but many older buildings have fallen into disrepair.

The Roman Catholic church at the Valley, Anguilla
(B&U Int. Picture Service)

"Modern traditional" architecture in tourist mecca, Philipsburg, Sint Maarten
(KIT Picture Library)

St. Vincent & the Grenadines

Guadeloupe, Martinique

Trinidad & Tobago

St. Lucia

Harbor and parliament
building (with Big Ben) at
Bridgetown, Barbados
(B&U Int. Picture Service)

Central library in Derek
Walcott Square, Castries,
St. Lucia
(B&U Int. Picture Service)

Grenada

Sint Maarten

American Virgin Islands

Barbados

Catholic church in Fort-de-France. In the foreground a statue commemorates Martinicans who died at Verdun in the First World War
(J.P.Lafont/Sygma)

Ramshackle Roseau, the capital of Dominica
(Philip Wolmuth)

Market in the main square of Basse-Terre, Guadeloupe
(Wheeler/ABC Press)

French cars and communications in Fort-de-France, Martinique
(David Simson/B&U)

Dominica

British Virgin Islands

Anguilla

Monserrat

Older houses in St. John's, Antigua
(B&U Int. Picture Service)

18th-century stone buildings
and original roof tiles in St.
George's, Grenada
(Philip Wolmuth)

Oil storage tanks tower over
Laventille in Port of Spain,
one of the Trinidadian
capital's poorer areas
(Philip Wolmuth)

anachronistic, activity in Barbados, St. Kitts, Trinidad & Tobago and the French islands.

In St. Kitts the pretty patchwork of canefields which slopes gently from the central mountain towards the sea belies the almost permanent crisis within the industry. Nationalized in 1975, the sugar sector accounts for as much as 40 per cent of the island's exports and a quarter of the workforce. The 20,000 tons which the island produces annually go mostly to Europe at a guaranteed price, but even this has not prevented the St. Kitts Sugar Manufacturing Corporation from incurring debts of $15 million. Hurricane Luis caused nearly $10 million of damage in 1995, ripping up railroad lines and destroying machinery. Unable to meet its quota to the EU, the Corporation had to import cheap sugar from Guatemala. To make matters worse, many Kittitians are unwilling to work in the industry, where they say pay and conditions are unacceptably poor. In 1996, the St. Kitts government imported 400 laborers from Guyana, who were prepared to accept $50-60 per week to cut cane.

In Barbados, the situation is equally serious. By 1993 production had fallen to 49,000 tons from average 1960s figures of 200,000 tons. Like St. Kitts, Barbados could not meet its EU quota (worth $25 million) and also had to make up the shortfall with sugar from Guatemala. Heavily indebted, the Barbados Sugar Industry Ltd. went into receivership in 1992, and the British company, Booker-Tate, took over management of the industry. A drastic restructuring plan was proposed, including the closure of one of the island's three refining mills. But even these moves could not prevent production dropping further in 1995 to only 38,000 tons. Many producers simply gave up on sugar and tried to sell their land for housing or tourism development.

Sugar exports from the Eastern Caribbean are only made viable by preferential trading agreements, and almost no sugar from the region is traded on the notoriously unstable world market. Under the terms of the Lomé Convention of 1975, signed between the countries of the European Economic Community (now European Union) and 46 former European colonies known as the African-Caribbean-Pacific (ACP) group, certain agricultural exports were guaranteed preferential access to the European market. For the Eastern Caribbean sugar-producers, this means that the EU undertakes to buy a certain tonnage of sugar at a price equivalent to that paid to European producers. Countries are allocated quotas for which they will receive the agreed price. At present, Barbados is entitled to export 54,000 tons, Trinidad & Tobago 44,000 and St. Kitts & Nevis 20,000 tons.

But this system is unlikely to provide long-term security for the region's sugar industry. The fourth Lomé Convention, signed in 1990, is due to expire at the end of 1999, and it is not clear whether the preferential system will be maintained thereafter.

The U.S. also imports some sugar from the region at above-market prices although the large U.S. sugar multinationals such as Amstar do not operate in the Eastern Caribbean. Quotas are determined by the U.S. Department of Agriculture and are meant to support high-cost regional producers while protecting domestic producers with guaranteed high prices. In 1995/6 quotas of 12,311 tons were allocated to Trinidad & Tobago and Barbados and 7,258 to St. Kitts & Nevis.

Sugar also survives because of its role in the more profitable rum industry. Almost every island manufactures rum, and the EU and U.S. are the principal export markets. In 1996 the EU agreed to offer a 1.3 million-gallon preferential quota to the English-speaking Caribbean for its "traditional" or dark rum, while rum from Martinique and Guadeloupe enters France at a reduced level of duty. In some cases, sugar production has been inadequate to supply the needs of local distillers, and they have been forced to buy in sugar from other countries.

Green Gold

The advent of the banana as the region's main export crop can be traced to the decline of the sugar industry and the need for alternative crops. The social unrest of the 1930s and the economic havoc wrought by the Second World War added new urgency to the search for new exports, at a time when technological advances in shipping and distribution allowed tropical fruit to be transported to distant markets. For the British government, eager to avoid the dependency and poverty associated with a bankrupt sugar industry, bananas seemed a promising alternative, and several commissions in the 1930s and 1940s proposed establishing an industry in the Eastern Caribbean.

Bananas offered several advantages both to the colonial authorities and to small farmers. They do not require large capital investment and can be grown by smallholders on hilly terrain unsuitable for other crops. They mature quickly and provide a regular cash income, ripening all year round. Although vulnerable to hurricanes, they can be replanted and productive again within six months. For the British, worried by the prospect of a potentially mutinous peasantry, the banana industry held out the prospect of moderate prosperity and social peace.

The British government established a guaranteed market for the region's banana exports by introducing a special licensing arrangement in 1952. This allowed so-called "sterling" bananas from the Caribbean to enter Britain duty-free, while "dollar" bananas from Latin America were subject to a quota and to duties. The arrangement encouraged Geest, a British-based company specializing in fruit and flowers, to enter the banana business,

Cutting bananas, St. Lucia

Philip Wolmuth

confident of a guaranteed market. Geest signed deals with the banana grow-ers' associations on the four Windward Islands of Dominica, Grenada, St. Lucia and St. Vincent and began shipping bananas to Britain in two small rented boats on a weekly basis.

During its four decades of business in the Eastern Caribbean Geest grew into a large and normally profitable company, increasing its turnover from £4 million in 1950 to £451 million in 1986. When conditions were good, the growers also did well, and the 1980s saw a gradual increase in banana earnings in the islands. But there were complaints that the growers took all the risks involved in banana production, but received only a small percent-age of the profits. In 1987 it was calculated that banana farmers received less than ten per cent of the fruit's final retail value and that Geest, by con-trolling shipping, distribution and ripening, made substantial profits at sev-eral different stages of the process. The system only worked because the British market – and to an extent the price – was guaranteed.

Britain's entry into the EEC in 1973 did not affect its relationship with the Windward Islands, and the Lomé Convention two years later reinforced the special treatment accorded to Caribbean bananas under the terms granted to the ACP countries. They entered Britain duty-free, while "dollar" ba-nanas continued to be subject to a twenty per cent duty. Other European nations had similar arrangements with their former colonies or overseas dependencies – France with Martinique and Guadeloupe, Italy with Somalia, Spain with the Canary Islands. Some, however, such as Germany, imported "dollar" bananas on the open market and paid a much lower price than that paid to the ACP producers.

The situation remained stable until 1992 when the EU moved towards the creation of a Single European Market, in which all trade barriers between member states were to be dismantled. This meant that the individual country-specific trading arrangements had to be scrapped and that, in theory, bananas imported into one EU state could be re-exported into another without quota restrictions or duties. The Eastern Caribbean governments realized that their bananas would have to compete with cheaper "dollar" bananas unless some sort of protection was maintained.

In the following years the EU has tried to create a "banana regime" which defends the interests of traditional ACP suppliers without discriminating against large Latin American producers. It has sought to maintain a guaranteed quota system, whereby the Windward Islands (and other ACP countries) are allocated a certain tonnage, while the rest of the EU's demand is met by "dollar" imports. Any imports over an agreed limit are liable to a high level of duty. The compromise has come under increasing attack, especially from U.S.-owned multinational corporations such as Chiquita which perceive the banana regime as an illegal obstacle to fair trade. They have managed to gain an increasing share of the European market, partly by buying interests in ACP producer countries and partly by over-supplying the European market to bring down prices. Many small producers believe that Chiquita intends to take control of the Windwards Islands industry, either by offering famers better prices or by precipitating a crisis in the existing export system.

The industry is now almost bankrupt. Prices in British supermarkets fell from around 50p/lb ($.80/lb) in the early 1990s to a low of 19p/lb ($0.30/lb) in late 1995. The producers were receiving payments from Geest which did not even cover their costs of production. There were strikes and riots in St. Lucia in 1994, and a series of storms and hurricanes across the region merely worsened conditions.

The real problem is that Eastern Caribbean producers cannot compete with the large plantation-based exporters of countries such as Colombia or Honduras. The small farmers of an island like Dominica typically work on holdings of an acre or so, often on steep hillsides, with family labor and limited technology. Companies such as Chiquita or Dole, on the other hand, control plantations of thousands of acres, with streamlined transport and a permanent labor force. Their costs per ton of bananas are far lower than those of small Caribbean farmer and they can supply European importers much more cheaply and reliably.

Finally, in late 1995, after several years of poor trading figures, Geest decided to sell its banana business and pull out of the Eastern Caribbean altogether. After months of uncertainty, the rival group Fyffes, in partnership with the Windward Islands Banana Development and Exporting Co (Wibdeco), a company co-owned by the four Windward Island governments, bought Geest out for $226 million. While this move gave the islands' producers a reprieve, it is still increasingly apparent that the expiry of the fourth Lomé Convention in 1999 will end existing preferences and usher in a free-market system. Few believe that the region's small farmers can survive such a transition.

Diversification

The banana crisis has intensified the search for other crops and commodities with which to rebuild an export economy. For years, regional governments have discussed diversification – alternative exports and alternative markets – but little has actually been achieved. In St. Lucia some farmers have abandoned bananas in favor of dairy-production and cut-flowers, and Dominica has started limited exports of passionfruit. Guadeloupe has moved into large-scale melon production, and Martinique exports pineapples. Some islands already have a more diversified agricultural economy. In Grenada,

for instance, bananas account for only about ten per cent of exports, and farmers also grow cocoa and nutmeg for overseas markets. St. Vincent, too, has other export commodities, including coconuts and arrowroot – a plant used by manufacturers of computer paper.

But alternative crops do not in themselves solve the islands' export problems. In recent years, Grenada's nutmeg industry has been badly hit by a trade war with Indonesia, the world's other leading producer. Several crops have been affected by bad weather, disease, and pests, most notably the pink mealy bug which was responsible for extensive damage to cocoa and other crops in sev-

Sorting nutmeg, Grenada
Philip Wolmuth

eral islands in 1995 and 1996. More permanent is the problem of securing markets, since the islands cannot produce anything more cheaply than their larger competitors. Whatever the agro-export, small-island economies remain unhealthily dependent on foreign markets, transnational companies, and uncertain trends in consumer tastes and world prices.

Despite the problems of the sugar and banana industries, agriculture continues to provide a livelihood for hundreds of thousands of people in the islands. Most people in rural areas grow crops such as yams and bananas for personal consumption, and some small farmers produce for local needs. Every island has at least a weekly market in town, where producers, normally women, sell fruit and vegetables.

Some small farmers are more adventurous, seeking to sell their produce in other islands where there is greater demand. A growing number of women, known as "hucksters," carry fruit and vegetables from islands such as Dominica to such nearby destinations as Guadeloupe or the U.S. Virgin Islands, where the agricultural sector is much weaker. Traveling by small boat or airplane, they sell their produce and normally return with manufactured goods or clothes which they then sell locally. Dealing with foreign exchange rates, customs officials, and arduous traveling, the hucksters are a resilient community. With organizations in Dominica, Grenada, and St. Vincent, they have received valuable support with credit and marketing from European and North American development agencies.

Another mainstay of the rural economy is fishing, and several islands have received considerable grants and loans to develop their fishing industries. Japan has given St. Vincent several million dollars to develop a fisheries program and Kingstown now boasts a new fish market, known locally as "Little Tokyo." About 1,500 people in Grenada (five per cent of the workforce) are employed in fishing; Japan also financed new facilities in the Grenadian fishing communities of Gouyave and Grenville.

Manufacturing

After the 1983 invasion, the U.S. government tried to promote Grenada as the ideal location for foreign manufacturers to set up shop. An industrial park was built near the airport; a whole range of tax incentives was offered. The idea was to demonstrate to the region that free-market development, based on foreign investment, was superior to the mixed economy strategy pursued by the now defunct People's Revolutionary Government. At first, a few American companies came to the island: Johnson & Johnson, SmithKline Beecham, and a handful of others made pharmaceutical products such as contact lens cases and employed 200 people. But gradually, as the incentives dried up, the companies left, attracted by cheaper labor and greater proximity to the U.S. market in places such as Mexico or the Dominican Republic. These days, Grenada's biggest manufacturing plant is the local brewery.

Grenada's problems are shared by the other smaller islands. Their labor costs are too high; they are too far away from the U.S.; their domestic markets are too small to support significant local manufacturing. Only Trinidad, with its population of 1.3 million and oil and gas industries, has an extensive manufacturing sector. Since the advent of the North American Free Trade Agreement (NAFTA) in 1994, linking Mexico's cheap-labor economy to that of the U.S. and Canada, North American investors have largely bypassed the small islands of the Eastern Caribbean.

Nonetheless, some islands have managed to establish low-wage manufacturing sectors, specializing in clothing, sports goods and electronic components for the U.S. market. Some fourteen per cent of St. Lucia's workforce is employed in small assembly plants, making toys, sneakers and T-shirts for export. Tiny Montserrat exports electrical parts, and Dominica has a thriving company, Dominica Coconut Products, which exports over 3 million bars of soap each year. Martinique and Guadeloupe both have *zones industrielles* around their capitals, producing fertilizers, canned fruit, and soft drinks. Manufacturing, however, is mainly small-scale, aimed at the local market, and most islands have little more than a brewery, a rum distillery, a cement works, and perhaps a rice mill. Consequently, the demand for imported goods remains high. Most companies in the region are, in reality, little more than import-export agencies.

Boom and Bust

The economic "giant" of the region is Trinidad, and its fortunes have long depended on its oil industry and, more recently, on natural gas. Oil was first discovered in 1902, and foreign companies such as Shell and British Petroleum rushed to exploit the find and to set up refineries on the island to process crude oil from nearby Venezuela. The establishment of an oil industry attracted workers from other, smaller islands such as Grenada and created an organized, sometimes militant, working class, led by the Oilfields Workers Trade Union (OWTU). Workers at the refineries in Pointe-a-Pierre were at the forefront of the social unrest in the 1930s.

Even before offshore fields were found in 1955, oil had outstripped sugar as Trinidad's main economic activity. The industry created thousands of jobs and brought relative prosperity to the British colony, but most profits were repatriated to Europe or the U.S. Independence in 1962 brought Eric Williams' People's National Movement (PNM) to power, and within twelve years both BP and Shell had sold their interests to the government, perhaps fearful of political instability and attracted more by new finds in the North

Sea. The PNM government entered into a series of joint venture arrangements with U.S. corporations such as Tesoro, Texaco and Amoco, while founding its own Trinidad and Tobago Oil Company (Trintoc).

The 1970s were the golden years for Trinidadian oil. The Arab oil embargo and the resulting OPEC price rise in 1973 quadrupled the value of the island's petroleum overnight and led to what economist Clive Thomas estimates at $10 billion of windfall revenue. This money was largely raised from taxing the foreign multinational corporations. The island was literally awash with money, much of which disappeared into private bank accounts or extravagant government projects. The PNM built heavy industry plants at Point Lisas, hoping to diversify the economy into steel and chemicals production, while middle-class Trinidadians enjoyed a consumer spree of imported cars and televisions and trips to Miami. A popular calypso of the time was Mighty Sparrow's *Capitalism Gone Mad*, which satirized the "boom" and complained of high prices and corruption.

"Capitalism Gone Mad"

> **You have to be a millionaire**
> **Or some kind of petty bourgeoisie**
> **Anytime you living here in this country**
> **You have to be a sculduggery**
> **Making your money illicitly**
> **To live like somebody in this country.**
> **It's outrageous and insane**
> **The crazy prices here in Port of Spain...**
> **Where you ever hear a television costs seven thousand dollars?**
> **Quarter million dollars for a piece of land**
> **A pair of sneakers two hundred dollars**
> **Eighty to ninety thousand dollars for motor cars**
> **At last here in Trinidad we see capitalism gone mad...**

> *Francisco Slinger, aka The Mighty Sparrow*

By 1982 oil prices had collapsed and the party was over. Petrodollars which had subsidized government spending and encouraged borrowing dried up; between 1982 and 1989 Trinidad's GDP shrank every year. Production fell from 230,000 barrels per day in 1978 to 150,000 in 1988. The oil industry has never recovered from the setback, and current production of 130,000 bpd reflects low world prices. Worse, Trinidad's proven reserves of oil are limited to only twelve years at current production rates, although companies such as Exxon and Total are currently exploring for further fields. The future now lies more with natural gas, which is used to power heavy industries such as iron, steel, and petrochemicals like methanol and ammonia.

Tourism

When a jumbo jet lands at Point Salines airport in Grenada, it is quite literally the biggest thing on the island. The arrival of one or two cruise ships in St. John's Antigua, dwarfs the surrounding buildings, making the port look like a toy model. The luxurious 196-room Four Seasons Resort on the island of Nevis, with its eighteen-hole golf course and choice of swimming pools, employs more people than the local government.

Tourism is the world's fastest growing industry and it is big business in the Eastern Caribbean. Every island, from Saba (28,000 arrivals in 1994) to St. Martin (585,000), from Montserrat (21,000) to Martinique (366,000) is involved in the industry, and some are absolutely dependent on it.

Trinidad oil worker   *Philip Wolmuth*

Tourism brings foreign exchange, employment, and economic growth. In 1994 tourists spent $50 million in St. Vincent, $75 million in St. Kitts, more than $200 million in St. Lucia and more than $300 million in Antigua and Barbados. In several countries – Antigua, Barbados, Grenada and St. Kitts – tourism earnings outweighed all other exports and services combined in value. The percentage of the workforce involved in the industry varies from 25 per cent (Antigua) to less than ten per cent (Dominica). Moreover, for every official job in a hotel or tourist office there are many more informal sector jobs, ranging from taxi-driving to selling trinkets on the beach.

Every island tries to promote its own attractions in a very competitive marketplace. Some offer traditional "sun, sea and sand" packages, with the emphasis on beach activities; others appeal to a more up-market clientele with eco-tourism and "heritage" tourism. Some aim for high numbers of visitors and have encouraged extensive hotel construction to accommodate them; others aspire to lower arrival figures but higher per capita expenditure. Everywhere the goal is to persuade the tourist to spend as much as possible.

The growing popularity of cruises has added to the numbers arriving in the islands, but locals complain that passengers stay only a couple of hours and spend little money. Since the huge vessels operated by companies like Royal Caribbean Cruise Lines contain their own restaurants, bars, and duty-free shops, the tourists have little incentive to spend money ashore. There are also arguments between governments and cruise ship companies over taxes to be paid for the use of port facilities and the alleged dumping of waste into the sea.

All-Inclusives or Exclusives

In 1994 Antiguans were either amused or indignant to read that their prime minister, Lester Bird, had been refused entry into Club Antigua by an over-zealous security guard for not having a pass. The hotel in question is one of the growing number of so-called all-inclusive resorts, where tourists pay in advance not only for their accommodation, but for all food, drink, and entertainment. Once inside the perimeter fence of the hotel grounds there is no need to leave until it is time to return to the airport. It is also difficult, critics say, for anyone from the island, even the prime minister, to gain access to the hotel.

The first all-inclusives belonged to the Club Med chain, but currently the most successful companies are Sandals and Super Clubs, owned by Jamaican entrepreneurs. All-inclusives now operate in almost every island in the region apart from Trinidad, Dominica, and some of the smallest territories.

Critics point out that all-inclusives reduce the amount of money that the rest of the economy can make from tourism, since everything is pre-paid and tourists do not need to buy meals or drinks outside. They also complain that these resort hotels import most of their food and equipment from abroad, mostly the U.S., hence failing to provide work or income for local farmers or manufacturers. The fact that locals are denied access to beaches and hotel grounds is also a source of resentment. When Princess Diana stayed at the $1,100 per night K-Club in Barbuda in 1995, for instance, the beach was closed to locals, creating considerable ill will.

The Offshore Sector

Small islands with few resources often have to find imaginative ways of bringing in revenue. For a while Saba attracted Dutch learner drivers (and $300,000 a year) with the promise of an easier driving test than in Holland. Dominica raised $7 million in the early 1990s by selling citizenship to investors from Taiwan and Hong Kong. St. Vincent has become a flag of convenience for merchant ships, registering 600 vessels by 1994. Some islands host offshore university facilities, where students from the U.S. study

Cruise ship tourists, Antigua
Philip Wolmuth

for qualifications which are sometimes of questionable value. Drugs have become part of the regional landscape, and the transshipment of cocaine from Latin America into the U.S. is reputed to bring millions of dollars into some islands.

More legitimate is the offshore data service industry, in which Barbados, St. Lucia and Dominica are involved. Improved technology and communications mean that typists in the islands can input, for considerably lower wages, the masses of figures generated by U.S. credit card companies, airlines and similar businesses. Barbados earned $41 million from the data-entry industry in 1993.

But the growth area in recent years has been offshore finance, including banks, insurance, and other services. The main beneficiaries of this growth have been the British colonies of Anguilla and Montserrat, whose political stability has attracted hundreds of companies, eager to minimize taxation and other costs by holding money in overseas accounts. While most transactions are legal, the offshore banks have also caught the eye of other, less reputable, clients. Money-laundering, principally on the part of drug cartels, has become a serious problem. In 1993, for instance, the British authorities in Anguilla set up a bogus bank, with the aim of trapping criminal investors. "Operation Dinero" led to the seizure of $50 million in assets, nine tons of cocaine, and a shipment of arms bound for Croatia.

Debt and Adjustment

The economic uncertainties of the 1980s and 1990s, together with prevailing free-market thinking, have forced many of the islands into programs of structural adjustment. An underlying problem is the amount of debt that some owe to foreign banks and international organizations like the World Bank and International Monetary Fund (IMF). Antigua, for instance, has one of the world's highest per capita debts at $4,500, due to government over-borrowing. Countries such as Trinidad & Tobago and Barbados are also seriously indebted and have trouble in meeting repayment schedules.

The debt problem has coincided with a decrease in aid and concessional lending from governments and international institutions. In 1995 Britain announced that it was abandoning bilateral aid to the islands and would henceforth fund only regional projects. The European Union provides funding for some development initiatives but cannot provide governments with budgetary support to meet their day-to-day commitments.

This has led to cuts in public spending, attempts to reduce the state-sector workforce and privatization programs across the region. During the 1990s the IMF has been active in Barbados, Dominica, Grenada and Trinidad & Tobago, lending money to relieve balance-of-payments crises if the governments agree to push through structural adjustment programs. The IMF recipe usually includes spending cuts, devaluation of currencies, and, wherever possible, the sale of state companies to private investors. As a result, Trinidad & Tobago has sold parts of its oil and gas sector to foreign companies, as well as privatizing state utilities such as electricity. Other islands have sold, or are trying to sell, state assets in banking, airlines, and tourism.

The imposition of pay freezes and redundancies has created tension in several countries, provoking public-sector strikes in 1995 in Barbados, Grenada, St. Lucia and Trinidad & Tobago. As further austerity is demanded by governments and the international financial institutions over coming years, industrial unrest – as well as more privatization – will remain a fact of life.

4   SOCIETY: THE WEIGHT OF HISTORY

To one side of *La Savane*, the once elegant park at the centre of Martinique's capital, Fort-de-France, stands a poignant reminder of the island's history. Amidst the stately lines of royal palm trees a white marble statue has been decapitated, the headless figure daubed with red paint. On the base somebody has scrawled in Creole *Respek a Matinik* ("Respect to Martinique"). The statue is that of Marie-Josèphe Rose Tascher de la Pagerie, better known as the Empress Joséphine and first wife of Napoleon Bonaparte. Born in colonial Martinique into a slave-owning white family, she became the most powerful woman in Europe until her divorce in 1806. But in Martinique she is remembered primarily (and, some say, mythically) as the influence behind Napoleon's decision to reintroduce slavery in the French Caribbean in 1802. Her family, it is said, had interests both in Martinique and Haiti and she was opposed to abolition, decreed eight years earlier by the revolutionary Convention.

The vandalism inflicted on Joséphine's statue may seem irrelevant to modern Martinique, but it reflects not only the persistence of anti-French and pro-independence feeling among certain Martinicans, but also an ancestral resentment against the so-called *békés*, the locally born whites who have traditionally held power in Martinique and of whom Joséphine has become a symbol. In terms of race, color, and language the legacy of Martinique's complex history endures.

A statue was also the center of a dispute in late 1995 in Barbados, an island not normally known for controversy. The Nelson statue in Bridgetown, long the symbol of British imperial force, came under attack as representing slavery and the suffering of black Barbadians. Nelson was an outspoken defender of slavery, claimed the statue's opponents, and as such should be removed. A song by the local calypsonian, Mighty Gabby, entitled *Take Down Nelson,* had already proved popular, and newspaper editorials argued over the issue.

Behind the mostly light-hearted war of words lay a more serious social concern: the continuing power exerted in the island's economy and society by a small sector of white Barbadians. Although political power has passed to black and colored leaders, the remnants of the old "plantocracy" along with more recent arrivals, still hold disproportionate influence in areas such as tourism and the retail sector. Professor Hilary Beckles of the University of the West Indies has written of a "new plantocracy," recreated by corporate ownership of the tourism industry and based on the old merchant-planter elite.

Stability and Tensions

In many respects the islands of the Eastern Caribbean are a social success story. Most have enjoyed decades of stable multi-party democracy and gradually improving living standards. The "slums of empire" are long gone and, with the exception of Grenada in 1979 and Trinidad's abortive coup attempts, there has been little of the social unrest to be found in other parts of the developing world.

Barbados, for instance, is now one of the region's richer nations, with annual per capita income of more than $11,000 rivalling that of Greece or Portugal. Trinidad & Tobago ranks 36th in the World Bank's economic league table of 132 nations. Islands such as Antigua, St. Kitts & Nevis and St. Lucia have recently been promoted from the World Bank's "lower middle income" category to that of "upper middle income." Only Dominica, Grenada and St. Vincent remain in the former grouping.

Most territories boast impressive social indicators. Literacy in Barbados is officially estimated at 98 per cent, in Trinidad & Tobago at 95 per cent, in Guadeloupe and St. Kitts at 90 per cent. Only in some of the smaller and poorer islands like St. Vincent does it drop to 80-85 per cent. Life expectancy throughout the islands averages well over 70 years, and infant mortality rates are between 10 and 20 per 1,000 live births, almost matching that of the U.S. Most islands have well-equipped hospitals, a network of primary and secondary schools, and a modern infrastructure of roads and communications.

In some cases, the social welfare enjoyed by people in the region is the result of subsidies from elsewhere. It has been estimated that the annual per capita GDP of Martinique and Guadeloupe would fall from over $4,000 to about $800 without the billions of francs spent on the islands each year by the French government. Equally, the territories of the Netherlands Antilles are dependent on direct subsidies from The Hague worth $100 million annually to fund their social services.

Yet this level of social welfare is now threatened by the imposition of structural adjustment programs across the region, aimed at reducing state spending and indebtedness. In the course of the 1990s, every government has been obliged to introduce austerity packages and cuts in social services. Traditionally, the state has been an important employer in small islands, offering jobs in the civil service, education and health, and public-sector companies. The need to cut budget deficits and government payrolls has pushed many politicians towards privatization and redundancy programs.

The most tangible consequence of such policies has been worsening unemployment. Unemployment rates of twenty per cent or more have been recorded in Barbados and Trinidad & Tobago in recent years. Even in the subsidized societies of Martinique and Guadeloupe, the percentage out of work in late 1995 was 26.9 per cent and 26.3 per cent respectively. Few islands can afford adequate social security or unemployment benefit, and an extended period out of work can bring real poverty.

Nor does the relative social stability enjoyed by most islands mean that inequalities and divisions have been eradicated. On the contrary, the countries of the Eastern Caribbean are split by many of the faultlines – race-, class-, and gender-based – which threaten social cohesion in other parts of the world. In some places ethnic differences are still potentially explosive, while in others extremes of wealth and poverty exacerbate tensions.

Black and White

White rule in the Caribbean is now largely a thing of the past. The economic power of the planter class was gradually eroded in the century following abolition, and many families from the local elites abandoned their plantations. But in some islands, a numerically insignificant minority continues to wield considerable economic influence. In Barbados, the department stores which line Bridgetown's Broad Street are mostly in white hands, and the import-export sector is reputedly dominated by a handful of white families. Resentment occasionally surfaces, as in the 1986 General Election when a senior member of the Barbados Labour Party defected to the opposition, accusing his former party of being controlled by white business interests.

In Martinique, and to a lesser degree in Guadeloupe, there is occasionally open hostility between the black majority and a small white minority. As recently as the 1950s, a French writer could describe the Martinican *békés* as "an exclusive caste made up of a dozen or so families including at the most a thousand individuals who see eye to eye, help each other financially, take care to preserve the plantations undivided, marry within their circle." In the exclusive Fort-de-France suburb of Didier, elaborate and well-tended nineteenth-century mansions testify to their once legendary social status. While the *békés* may be a waning force, tensions between black Martinicans and whites are still acute. Sometimes tourists from France or elsewhere are the targets of abuse, but real resentment is directed against French nationals who allegedly monopolize the best jobs in the state sector. Known pejoratively as *zoreilles* (perhaps because of their sunburnt ears), the incoming whites are perceived by many as forming a new ruling caste.

Here and elsewhere, racism takes many different and pervasive forms. According to the Guadeloupean sociologist, Michel Giraud, "white is from every point of view synonymous with everything that is good, and black with everything that is bad." In every island, those with lighter skins tend to dominate the higher echelons of society, whether in the professions or business. While no official segregation or color bars exist, there is nevertheless a correlation between skin color and social class. This "pigmentocracy" may not exclude all blacks from positions of power (and in most islands there is a black elite), but it certainly favors those with lighter skin.

Divide and Rule

Some of the worst racial conflict in the region has been found in Trinidad, where people of East Indian descent (40 per cent) outnumber Afro-Trinidadians (37 per cent). Since indentureship brought 145,000 immigrants from India to the island to replace black slave labor, the interests of this group have often clashed with those of the blacks. This was partly intended: the British colonial authorities wished to minimize militancy among the agricultural labor force by following a "divide and rule" policy. For decades black Trinidadians derided the "coolies" for accepting low wages and doing the dirty work of cane-cutting. The two communities remained stubbornly separate and mutually suspicious; inter-marriage was almost unknown and violence was commonplace. While many East Indians have remained in agriculture up to the present day, others have built up businesses with their savings and gradually formed a distinct middle class, specializing in law, medicine, and commerce.

With independence, Afro-Trinidadians assumed political power and dominated the important state-run petroleum industry. Few East Indians found jobs in this sector, and rural communities of Indian descent remained alienated from Port of Spain and its black political leadership. When in 1970 a "Black Power" uprising threatened the government, East Indians refused to join anti-government actions, finding no common cause with the young black radicals.

Voting in elections has invariably taken place along racial lines, and this remains the case today. Attempts to create non-ethnic political parties or to build multi-ethnic alliances have always failed. The National Alliance for Reconstruction which came to power in 1986 rapidly disintegrated amid accusations of racism. Basdeo Panday's electoral victory in November 1995 created Trinidad's first East Indian prime minister, yet by no means spelt the end of racial politics or conflict.

Women

Women in the Eastern Caribbean tend to have greater economic and social autonomy than in most other parts of the world. Sociologists believe that the double legacy of slavery and migration has partly created the social attitudes which lead to the region's popular image of the tough, independent woman. During slavery women worked alongside men as field laborers and after emancipation continued to share agricultural labor either on the plantation or in smallholdings. Slave-owners discouraged stable marriages, leading to large numbers of female-headed households, a phenomenon

Trinidadian girls

Hulton Getty

reinforced by large-scale male migration. Today, approximately 35 per cent of households in the Eastern Caribbean are headed by women.

Women are still the motor of the region's agricultural economy. They frequently play the double role of farmer and market trader, working long hours in both field and marketplace. A large percentage of smallholdings throughout the Eastern Caribbean are worked by women, particularly in areas where male migration is high. Statistics suggest that women make up between 30 and 50 per cent of the agricultural workforce in all of the English-speaking islands.

Most jobs in manufacturing plants are also held by women, who are preferred to men by employers for their alleged dexterity and ability to cope with long hours. They are typically paid twenty per cent less than their male counterparts and are considered less likely to join trade unions. But the bulk of female employment is to be found in the service sector, whether in tourism, commerce or, most importantly, domestic work. Much of this work is casual, with few rights or privileges. Paid vacations, sick leave, and job security are rare.

Women face discrimination in many areas of everyday life. In farming, for instance, they find it more difficult than men to gain access to credit – the lifeblood of every smallholding – often because their names do not appear on title deeds. Market traders and "hucksters" often encounter hostility from tax and customs officialdom, which tends to see their work as "black market". Women workers are more likely to be unemployed than men; unemployment figures from Barbados in 1995 showed male and female unemployment at 17.7 per cent and 23.4 per cent respectively. A similar pattern of discrimination exists in the French *départements d'outre-mer*, where unemployment remains stubbornly high.

Teenage pregnancies are a serious problem throughout the region, and significant numbers of single mothers are under twenty years old. In many cases, they have to rely on their own mothers for support, placing an extra burden on them. In Martinique and Guadeloupe, no fewer than 50 per cent of young women between fifteen and nineteen have children. According to some sociologists, this provides them with status, an alternative to unemployment, and access to social security payments.

Women are also under-represented in positions of influence and political power. Former Prime Minister Eugenia Charles of Dominica and the late Governor-General of Barbados, Dame Nita Barrow, are exceptions to the rule that politics is dominated by men. Women generally hold less than a quarter of elected positions in the region's parliaments, with only Grenada reaching 27 per cent. In the French islands, women make up only fifteen per cent of elected officials, mostly at municipal rather than regional level.

Yet there are signs that women may soon be able to improve their social and economic status. Figures released by the University of the West Indies in late 1995 showed that women constituted 60 per cent of the student population, outnumbering men in every faculty apart from engineering. This confirmed evidence that girls are now more likely to stay on at school and complete their secondary education than boys.

Young and Old

For those unable to continue through the education system, life on a small island can be far from idyllic. With few training opportunities and no access to credit, young people often face the boredom and frustration of long-term unemployment. In Trinidad & Tobago unemployment among the 15-19 age group is currently estimated at around 45 per cent. In Martinique and Guadeloupe, the figures stand at 70 per cent for the same age-group, and young people who have never worked have no entitlement to unemployment benefit. The worst incidence of unemployment is to be found in rural areas, where few young people relish the idea of a lifetime's hard work on a small farm.

Life expectancy has improved dramatically in the last half century, and most people in the Eastern Caribbean can anticipate living into their seventies. Yet old age can bring insecurity, especially in the poorer islands where pensions are inadequate or nonexistent. Family support networks are important, with women playing the major role in caring for elderly relatives. Remittance payments sent from abroad by children are also a vital source of income, and Church-based charities provide occasional hand-outs.

The Urban-Rural Divide

Most Eastern Caribbean islands are still largely rural in character, with the majority of people living in villages or scattered communities. But this is rapidly changing, as job opportunities, social services and recreational activity are increasingly concentrated in towns and cities. From their outset as colonial trading stations, the islands have tended to look towards the capital, invariably a port, as the center of social and economic life. This has continued into the present day, with government offices, shopping centers and hospitals normally situated in the main town and its suburbs.

As a result, people are gradually moving away from rural areas, in search of work and services. In some territories such as St. Vincent and Dominica, with strong traditions of village life, this is less pronounced. But in Trinidad & Tobago, 65 per cent of people live in Port of Spain and the other main towns of San Fernando and Arima. In St. Lucia the urban population of 45 per cent is concentrated in Castries, where ugly concrete tenements have replaced much of the capital's 18th-century architecture. The highest urban population is to be found in Martinique, where over 50 per cent of people live in the Fort-de-France area, reflecting the importance of state-sector jobs to the economy.

Suburbs and Shanties

Within the towns there are huge discrepancies between the middle-class and elite suburbs and the poor districts. The pleasantly leafy Port of Spain residential area of Maraval, with its golf course and half-timbered English-style homes, is a world removed from the grim squalor of Laventille, where tumbledown shacks cling onto an overcrowded hillside. Some sixteen per cent of Trinidadians live in squatter settlements on state-owned land without access to water or electricity, according to the government. In Fort-de-France, the luxurious villas of the rich and the modern apartment blocks of the middle classes stand in contrast to *bidonvilles* or shanties such as Volga Plage, more reminiscent of Haiti than of France.

There are pockets of extreme poverty, even in some of the wealthier islands. Many tourists arriving in Antigua, St. Kitts or St. Lucia are surprised to learn that whole families live in small wooden houses with primitive sanitation and few amenities. Some rural districts in Grenada and Dominica are particularly marginalized, and the impoverished northeast of St. Vincent, where there are still a few "black Carib" communities, electricity is only just arriving.

Collecting water from a standpipe, St. Lucia   *Philip Wolmuth*

When wages are low or nonexistent and building materials such as wood and cement are expensive, it is often impossible for poorer families to improve their living conditions. At election time, politicians promise better water or electricity supplies, but such pledges rarely materialize. Some governments have invested in low-cost housing schemes, moving families out of slums, but housing remains a serious problem throughout the region. The regular ravages inflicted by hurricanes aggravate the situation.

Drugs and Crime

Faced with low incomes and few long-term prospects, a minority of people, mostly young and male, resort to crime. One fertile area for criminal activity is the tourism industry, where relatively wealthy foreign visitors make tempting targets. Violent crime is still very uncommon in the Eastern Caribbean (in some small islands like Saba or Anguilla it is virtually unknown), but muggings and robberies have increased in places such as St. Lucia and Barbados.

Tourism also encourages a subculture of informal-sector activity which includes begging, hustling, and, more seriously, drug-dealing. Marijuana is widely available throughout the islands and is extensively cultivated in Trinidad and St. Vincent. Tourists are perceived as a lucrative market for ganja and can expect to be hassled by would-be dealers.

Much more serious is the impact of cocaine and crack on the region. *Time* magazine reported in 1996 that several islands, including Trinidad, St. Lucia, Antigua and St. Kitts, were in danger of being overrun by drug traffickers who use them as transshipment points for cocaine en route to the U.S. The magazine alleged that high-ranking officials in Trinidad had connections with drug cartels and that drug-related violence had given St. Lucia the second highest murder rate in the world. Other reports from the United Nations and the U.S. State Department have also pinpointed St. Vincent, Antigua and St. Kitts as major transshipment centers.

The case of St. Kitts demonstrates how vulnerable a small society can be to organized crime. In late 1994 a series of murders, including that of the Deputy Prime Minister's son, shocked the island. The head of St. Kitts' special branch, who was investigating the killings, was also assassinated. In subsequent police enquiries, in which Scotland Yard was involved, it was revealed that the murders were linked to large consignments of cocaine deposited on the island for subsequent transport to the U.S. Locals had long suspected that unusual night-time activity around the mostly deserted southeastern peninsula had sinister motives.

Drug money is by its nature hard to quantify, but the luxury homes and new BMWs to be seen on several islands are symptoms of its presence. Cocaine is also more easily available, as some intermediaries are paid in kind. This has created further problems of addiction and violence between rival gangs. Although all governments strenuously deny it, the U.S. State Department alleges corruption and complicity in the highest echelons of society.

Migration

Since the nineteenth century, people from the Eastern Caribbean have been on the move, in search of work and a better future away from their home islands. Some 20,000 men, or 40 per cent of the adult male population, left Barbados between 1881 and 1914 to work on the Panama Canal, along with large numbers from the French islands. Workers from St. Kitts and Anguilla went to cut sugar-cane in the Dominican Republic (there are still English-speakers in some sugar areas) or Cuba. The oil industry in Trinidad, Aruba, and Curaçao drew workers from Grenada and other islands during the 1950s and 1960s. More recently, the relative affluence of Guadeloupe and Martinique has attracted migrants from neighboring Dominica and St. Lucia.

The Cold North

The great exodus of migrants to Britain began in the 1950s, when cheap labor was needed to help in post-War reconstruction. Every island saw large numbers of its people, mostly young men, board the ships which would

On the move, Barbados airport   *Philip Wolmuth*

deposit them weeks later at Southampton or Tilbury docks. Jobs were available in the public sector, notably in transport and the health service, and in industries such as car-manufacturing. Altogether, some 250,000 people from the Caribbean, a large proportion from Jamaica, arrived in Britain before the 1962 Commonwealth Immigration Act limited entry.

People from the smaller islands formed communities, sometimes in unlikely places. Migrants from St. Vincent settled in numbers in High Wycombe, about 20 miles outside London. Anguillans opted for the town of Slough, where they worked in light engineering. Slough was then in Buckinghamshire (it is now in Berkshire) and the money sent back to Anguilla was popularly known as "Sloughbucks." Grenadians favored Huddersfield, Barbadians established communities in Birmingham and Manchester. Despite community support, many immigrants encountered low wages, poor housing, and racism.

When further legislation in 1968 and 1971 closed Britain to large-scale migration, the U.S. and Canada took its place as the migrants' goal. From the 1960s onwards thousands of people, often young women, left for New York, Miami or Toronto. Today, there are more people from Nevis or Anguilla in New York than remain on the islands. Each island has its associations and clubs, and migrants retain a strong sense of identity. Brooklyn is the center of the English-speaking Caribbean community in New York, and its annual Carnival, with steelbands and calypso, has attracted crowds of up to a million.

Migration and the remittances sent home by workers overseas have acted as a safety valve in many of the islands, reducing unemployment and poverty. But it is often the best qualified, most enterprising people who leave, creating a shortage of skilled and professional workers. Many migrants eventually return home with their savings in order to set up a business or to retire.

The Community Response

Crime and migration are two responses to poverty and unemployment, but some communities and organizations have found alternative strategies for survival. Traditional cooperative savings and credit schemes date back to the rise of an independent peasantry in the nineteenth century, and many communities have a tradition of sharing certain work like house-building or harvesting. The islands' churches have often been instrumental in fostering a sense of community and, in many cases, are the main support for those in real difficulty.

A range of non-governmental organizations (NGOs) are also active in the Eastern Caribbean, providing funds and support for local and regional initiatives. With resources from Europe or North America, NGOs are keen to develop grassroots development projects which will benefit those most at risk from economic and social deterioration. In islands like Dominica and St. Lucia, heavily dependent on the threatened banana industry, local groups are working with small farmers to explore the possibilities for crop diversification. Elsewhere, women are given particular priority in education, training, and legal aid schemes.

While large grants from donors such as the European Union often go direct to governments for infrastructural projects, it is also possible for NGOs to divert resources to smaller-scale community programs. Here the emphasis is on building local leadership and providing the capital to allow people to start up small businesses or farming ventures. In Grenada, for instance, a local NGO is behind a car mechanics' workshop which trains unemployed young men, a small furniture factory, a pre-school nursery, and a spice-packaging plant.

Regional organizations such as the Barbados-based Caribbean Conference of Churches and the Caribbean Policy Unit also play an important role in bringing local agencies together within the wider context. Links with the University of the West Indies, both in Barbados and Trinidad, allow NGOs access to data and technology which helps them coordinate their work. Their role in advising governments and local financial institutions is becoming more important, especially in the areas of rural development and women's issues.

5   CULTURE: CREATION AND CELEBRATION

One of the Eastern Caribbean's most spectacular sights is the Pitons, two volcanic peaks which emerge from the sea on St. Lucia's south-west coast. The twin peaks are steep-sided, densely forested and rise almost 3,000 feet above a sweeping valley which leads down to the sea. The area is not merely beautiful, but is considered of special natural and archaeological interest. Relics of the island's indigenous Arawak population have been found there, and evidence suggests that it was a holy place, where gods were worshiped among the natural grandeur.

A plan to build a hotel between the Pitons in the late 1980s met with hostility and incredulity from conservationists, who claimed that it would ruin the site and destroy its eco-system. Nevertheless, planning permission was granted, and in 1992 Jalousie Plantation Resort and Spa, financed by a Swiss corporation, opened its doors to those tourists willing to pay $400 daily for its all-inclusive luxury.

In the course of the controversy over Jalousie, public opinion was divided between some locals who welcomed new job opportunities and other St. Lucians who saw the plan as close to sacrilege. Most prominent among these was Derek Walcott, the poet and playwright who won the Nobel Prize for Literature in 1992. He attacked the scheme as a cynical exploitation of the Pitons, akin to opening "a casino in the Vatican" or "a take-away concession inside Stonehenge." In his speech at the Nobel Prize ceremony, Walcott spoke angrily of St. Lucia's transformation from a small agricultural society into a tourist mecca:

How quickly it could all disappear! And how it is beginning to drive us further into where we hope are impenetrable places, green secrets at the end of bad roads, headlands where the next view is not of a hotel but of some long beach without a figure and the hanging question of some fisherman's smoke at its far end. The Caribbean is not an idyll, not to its natives.

Walcott's concerns have been echoed by other writers, not just in St. Lucia but throughout the region. St. Lucian Earl Young's novel, *Consolation* (1994), describes how developers and investors arrive in a small rural community and build a tourist enclave which threatens the villagers' very identity:

Then came the bright, yellow bulldozers that shaved the slope as if the soil were as soft as ashes. They did not even hesitate at trees and rocks. The villagers came to watch, uncertain whether to be excited or frightened. The children welcomed the entertainment at first, with the boys all wishing to be tractor operators. Then they sensed their parents' unease and stopped coming.

Perhaps the most damning indictment of tourism's impact on the Eastern Caribbean is to be found in *A Small Place* (1988), Jamaica Kincaid's vitriolic account of Antigua's corruption. Addressing the newly-arrived tourist, Kincaid reveals the ugliness she sees at the heart of the Caribbean idyll:

> Oh, what beauty! You have never seen anything like this. You are so excited. You breathe shallow. You breathe deep. You see a beautiful boy, skimming the water, godlike, on a Windsurfer. You see an incredibly unattractive, fat, pastrylike-fleshed woman enjoying a walk on the beautiful sand, with a man, an incredibly unattractive, fat, pastrylike-fleshed man...

The advent of mass tourism and other forms of globalization is putting the culture of the Eastern Caribbean islands under strain. For writers such as Walcott, the authentic values of local culture – language, a sense of community, and history – are threatened by the relentless spread of North American materialism. As long ago as the 1960s the Trinidadian writer V.S. Naipaul lamented that the islands were selling themselves into a "new slavery" by rushing to embrace tourism.

But there is another point of view which argues that tourism's impact on culture is not all negative. The industry brings money, creates jobs, and keeps people in their communities. Tourist dollars enable some cultural forms such as festivals and music to survive and become better known outside the region. Many artists, craftspeople, and musicians depend on tourists to support their work.

The argument over tourism's influence is the latest episode in a longer-running debate over the real nature of local culture. The small islands' societies are the result of migration and mixing, the synthesis of people and culture from several continents. At different times, different parts of these complex societies have claimed to represent "real" cultural values, while other cultural forms have been dismissed and despised. Naipaul went so far as to state that the Caribbean was incapable of producing great art or literature. But the resilience of popular culture in its broadest sense, as opposed to European aesthetic ideals, has provided the region with some of its greatest achievements. These range from Trinidad's Carnival to the great West Indies cricket teams, from *soca* and *zouk* music to the islands' traditions of folk storytelling.

Colonial Legacies

The European powers left their mark on the islands in many ways. Education systems are still largely influenced by the experience of colonialism, and it is not long ago that children in the Caribbean wrote essays about snow at

The Pitons, St. Lucia   *Philip Wolmuth*

Christmas. The Church, whether Catholic or Protestant, has had a powerful impact through many generations and was closely connected to the colonial system of values. Other institutions – political, social, and cultural – owe much to European models.

But in many ways, the colonial system suppressed creativity among its subjects and taught them that local culture was inferior. The theme of imperial arrogance fills many of the region's novels, notably George Lamming's classic *In the Castle of My Skin* (1953), which pours scorn on the myth of "Little England." Likewise, Joseph Zobel's account of growing up in colonial Martinique, *Black Shack Alley* (1950), portrays the island's children as forced to mimic French values if they wish to get ahead. The stultifying atmosphere of 1940s Barbados was memorably described by traveler Patrick Leigh Fermor as reflecting "the social and intellectual values and prejudices of a Golf Club in Outer London."

In every island the impetus towards political reform and independence was accompanied by cultural challenges to the colonial status quo. Trinidad's famous calypso evolved into a medium for satirizing the authorities, and Carnival became an intense, albeit short-lived, vehicle for subverting the social hierarchy. Popular culture took shape in music, poetry, and painting and pushed against the restrictions of colonial society.

These forms were, to some extent, rooted in the experience of slavery and among the people, African and Indian, who had been brought to the plantations. The tradition of oral storytelling was transplanted from Africa, for example, and many tales, characters and phrases were transmitted from generation to generation for hundreds of years. The music and dances of the slaves were also African in inspiration, and most modern Caribbean music traces its roots back to the "Middle Passage." Religious and spiritual expressions are similarly resilient, having survived centuries of official censure.

Several external influences added to the development of such art forms in the 1940s and 1950s. The arrival of U.S. troops in islands like Antigua and Trinidad exposed locals to black American culture, including jazz and blues. The wider availability of radio and television in the following years increased awareness of popular culture elsewhere. Migration, whether to Europe, North America or other islands, brought people into contact with a range of experiences which affected their cultural outlook. In the 1950s a number of young writers, including Lamming and Naipaul, left to live and work in London. Exile allowed them to look at their own societies from a distance, either with affection or loathing. Others went to work in the oil refineries of Aruba or Curaçao and returned with the imprint of the Dutch Caribbean and Latin America.

Négritude

The political and cultural ferment of 1930s Paris created many artistic movements and theories. Among them was *négritude*, a term coined by the Martinican poet-politician, Aimé Césaire. The concept was largely a rejection of European cultural norms and a celebration of African or African-descended identity. Césaire and his followers believed that *la culture officielle* of Frenchness in Africa and the Caribbean had devalued all that was positive and creative about their majority black populations. It had forced France's colonial subjects to accept French ideas of what was "proper" culture. The solution, he believed, was to celebrate the exact qualities – sensuality, instinctiveness, irrationality – which Western rationalist thought condemned as barbarous. In his most famous poem, the epic *Return to My Native Land* (1939), Césaire condemns the age-old myth of white superiority ("for centuries Europe has stuffed us with lies and crammed us with plague") and rejoices in his own African identity and humanity:

do not make of me that man of hate for whom I have
only hate
I was born of this unique race
yet knowing my tyrannical love you know
it is not by hatred of other races that I prosecute for
mine.

All that I would wish is
to answer the universal hunger
the universal thirst

Césaire's writing became enormously influential among a generation of black intellectuals, and one of his disciples was Frantz Fanon, the Martinican psychiatrist who devoted his life to the Algerian war of liberation against France. In *Black Skin, White Masks* (1952), Fanon diagnosed what he saw as the black Martinican's inferiority complex as a repressive denial of his own Africanness.

Négritude has since been challenged by other literary theories such as *antillanité* and *créolité* which stress the importance of a specifically Caribbean, rather than African, cultural identity. Césaire has also been criticized by younger intellectuals for using classical French and not Creole – in itself, they say, a symptom of cultural assimilation.

The growth of black consciousness and the spread of radical ideas, influenced by thinkers such as Jamaica's Marcus Garvey, encouraged a revaluation of the region's history. Rejecting the Eurocentrism of traditional historians, writers such as Eric Williams and C.L.R. James stressed the role of black people in their own liberation from slavery and subsequent development. Williams, the long-serving prime minister of Trinidad & Tobago, contested the notion that abolition was granted on humanitarian grounds and argued that capitalist logic had rendered slavery inefficient and obsolete. The veteran Marxist, James, for a time in political sympathy with Williams, produced a number of works, including *The Black Jacobins* (1938), which analysed the interplay of race and class in the region's history.

The Literary Boom

Almost every island of the Eastern Caribbean has produced writers of international stature since the 1950s. Barbados can claim George Lamming and Kamau Brathwaite; Trinidad is the birthplace of V.S. and Shiva Naipaul and Samuel Selvon. Even the smaller islands have their own well-known names: Caryl Phillips (St. Kitts), Merle Collins (Grenada), Jamaica Kincaid (Antigua). Perhaps the most celebrated regional writer of recent years has been Derek Walcott, whose 1992 Nobel Prize followed the publication of his acclaimed *Omeros* (1990). In this reworking of Homeric legend, Walcott transposes the figures of classical Greece into the personae of contemporary St. Lucians, farmers and fishermen, whose Creole idioms are interwoven into the poem's lyricism.

A large number of successful writers have been women. Jean Rhys and Phyllis Shand Allfrey, both white women from Dominica, wrote haunting novels about the island's atmosphere of exoticism and menace. Rhys' *Wide Sargasso Sea* (1966) traces the descent into madness of Antoinette Cosway, the infamous mad first wife of Mr. Rochester in *Jane Eyre*. Similarly, Allfrey's *The Orchid House* (1953) uses Dominica's lush and sometimes sinister landscape as a background for the decline of a white island family and, by implication, the old colonial order. In Guadeloupe, too, women have eclipsed men in literature, even though the white male poet, Saint-John Perse, won the Nobel Prize for Literature in 1960. Both Maryse Condé and Simone Schwarz-Bart have been widely published and translated, and their historical novels of women's resilience have been highly successful.

In the French islands – and to a lesser extent, St. Lucia and Dominica – language itself is a serious issue. Some authors have refused to write in French, viewing it as an imposed and artificial medium, and have published novels in Creole. Others have incorporated Creole words and phrases into their French, hence enabling French readers to make sense of their work. Patrick Chamoiseau, who won the prestigious Prix Goncourt in 1992 with his novel *Texaco*, has succeeded in popularizing elements of Creole language and culture in France.

The Creole controversy underlines the fact that writers from the region are invariably dependent on publishers and readers in Europe or North America. As yet, there are only small local publishers, and books are often too expensive to reach a wide readership. In this respect, cultural dependency remains a problem.

Music

The best-known Caribbean music is probably Jamaican reggae or Cuban salsa, but the islands of the Eastern Caribbean have also produced some distinctive and very popular musical forms. *Zouk*, the music of Martinique and Guadeloupe, has spread throughout the other islands and to Europe. A synthesis of the 1930s *biguine* big band sound, Haitian *kadans ranpa* and U.S. black jazz, it incorporates various rhythms into an electronic mix, where synthesizers and drum machines imitate more traditional percussion instruments. The Guadeloupean band, Kassav', are the best-known exponents of the genre, which is most popular as dance music in the period surrounding carnival celebrations.

Trinidad is almost synonymous with calypso, a genre which reflects the island's mixed cultural heritage. A blend of French and African influences dating from the eighteenth century, calypso developed into a medium for social satire and ribaldry, where lyrics are much more important than in other popular forms. Although discouraged by the colonial authorities, it grew in popularity and became interlinked with Trinidad's other great cultural expression – Carnival.

The early decades of the twentieth century saw calypso transformed from its early, largely improvised, form into a more structured, text-oriented genre, which was performed to audiences in specially erected tents. The performers were contestants, pitting their wits against each other in pursuit of a prize. By the 1930s successful calypsonians (invariably men) were being recorded, but the colonial powers were increasingly concerned at the subversive tone of some of the songs. Censorship was strict, and calypsonians could be banned from performing. As the movement towards independence gathered pace, several calypsonians rose to prominence. The best-known was Mighty Sparrow (who is still performing today), whose support for Eric Williams' brand of nationalism was tempered by open ridicule of government incompetence.

Calypso's development ran parallel to the rise of steelband music, which began in the 1940s when it was discovered that empty oil drums, when dented in a special way, could produce an extraordinary range of tones. Groups were formed, and competition was fierce between rival "pan yards," where the music was played. Nowadays, pan music is a central part of Carnival, and bands are driven around Port of Spain on huge trailers at the height of the celebrations.

Calypso has remained the perfect medium for social satire, and few public figures escape mockery. But this means that it is very much a local phenomenon, since the lyrics are usually of little interest to a wider audience. Calypso has also come under fire from critics as being unacceptably sexist, with its denigration of women and celebration of macho values. The emergence of some women calypsonians such as Calypso Rose has only partly challenged the genre's traditional misogyny.

In the 1970s some younger musicians from Trinidad and other islands, tired of calypso's conventions, developed a faster, more dance-based, variant called *soca*. The 1983 hit, *Hot Hot Hot* by Montserrat's Arrow is probably the best example of the genre, which has now become distinct from the more sedate traditional calypso. There is now also an East Indian version of soca, called *chutney*, which took the 1996 Carnival by storm. But all local music faces stiff competition from rap, dancehall, and ragga, imported from the U.S. and Jamaica.

Carnival

"Up on the hill with Carnival coming, radios go on full blast, trembling these shacks, booming out calypsos, the songs that announce in this season the new rhythms for people to walk in, rhythms that climb over the red dirt and stone, break-away rhythms that laugh through the groans of these sights, these smells, that swim through the bones of these enduring people so that they shout: Life! They cry: Hurrah! They drink a rum and say: Fuck it!"
Earl Lovelace, *The Dragon Can't Dance*

Carnival is the focal point of Trinidad's entire year. The two rapturous days which precede Ash Wednesday in late February are the climax of the event, but Carnival lasts much longer than this, in anticipation and memory. From Christmas onwards, the songs which hope to win popular acclaim are heard on radio and in the calypso tents. At the same time, the organizers of the *mas* bands, the phalanxes of costumed marchers, work on the theme for this year's extravagant clothes and props.

Carnival procession, Trinidad

Philip Wolmuth

The essence of Carnival, apart from collective euphoria, is competition, and calypsonians struggle to impress a panel of judges who eventually select eight finalists to compete on Port of Spain's central Savannah park for the title of Calypso Monarch. Another less structured competition takes place the following day on Monday after the early morning *j'ouvert* revelers have splattered the unwary with paint or mud. Amidst the vast processions which move towards the Savannah, judges note the most popular songs played by steelbands and DJs, awarding the favorite the status of Road March of the year.

The *mas* bands, often numbering a thousand participants, are also in competition for the best and most spectacular theme. In recent years, Peter Minshall, a white Trinidadian, has been responsible for some of the most original and successful designs, which are worked on and paid for by some of Trinidad's poorest communities.

Some purists complain that Carnival has been taken over by commercial interests, which have tamed its subversive nature into an opportunity for sponsorship and advertising. But at least two-thirds of Trinidad's entire population still descends on Port of Spain each year for the cathartic combination of calypso, rum, and excitement.

Cricketing, a sporting obsession

Hansib Caribbean

Trinidad's Carnival is the giant among local festivals, but every island has its own way of celebrating. The rural villages of Guadeloupe and Martinique have their own *fêtes patronales*, with religious associations, and there are also carnival parades in the cities. Smaller islands like St. Vincent or St. Kitts have their own carnivals, while the Dutch territory of Sint Maarten has a major festival in April which attracts crowds of 100,000 people. St. Lucia's annual jazz festival is also developing a good reputation, drawing world-class performers and big audiences. The best event, however, is Barbados' Crop-Over, a two-week festival leading up to the first Monday in August. Originally the moment at which slaves celebrated the end of the sugar harvest, it almost disappeared in the 1940s but was resurrected in the 1970s as a tourist attraction with calypsos, parades and street fairs.

Cricket

In Guadeloupe and Martinique the national sports are cockfighting and horse racing; in the Dutch territories people prefer basketball or volleyball. But in the English-speaking Caribbean the sporting obsession is cricket, a game introduced by the British and perfected by local sportsmen. Football (soccer) is also hugely popular, and the region has produced world-class players such as Dwight Yorke (Trinidad) and Les Ferdinand (St. Lucia), but cricket is even more important. "Whoever and whatever we are," wrote C.L.R. James, "we are cricketers." As he and other observers have noted, the sport lies at the centre of the local male psyche.

Cricketing victories over England are particularly savored as sweet revenge against the former colonial masters. In a region where rivalries and divisions between islands have stood in the way of political progress, cricket has also been a unifying factor. The West Indies cricket team, created early in the twentieth century and open to players from all English-speaking islands, is a rare example of regional cooperation. At a local level, however, inter-island, and even inter-village, rivalries are fierce.

The bigger islands of Trinidad and Barbados can claim to be the regional centres of cricket, since they host international test matches and produce larger numbers of players for the West Indies team. But Antigua is also a major cricketing venue, and the other smaller islands all have national sides as well as hundreds of village teams. All young players who practise in village squares or urban backstreets, often without proper equipment, dream of joining the ranks of the region's greats. Modern-day heroes include Trinidad's Brian Lara, who scored a world record-breaking 501 runs in an English county match, and Antigua's Curtley Ambrose, ranking with legendary names from the past such as Viv Richards (Antigua), Gary Sobers (Barbados), and Learie Constantine (Trinidad). _D_

A string of bad results in recent years has created crisis in local cricket circles, prompting the resignations of players and calls to reform the selection procedure. The nadir came with defeat at the hands of unknown Kenya in the 1996 World Cup, creating outrage among supporters. In Barbados television coverage of the match was interrupted by a studio discussion on the need for a radical overhaul of the team's management.

WHERE TO GO, WHAT TO SEE

If it's beaches you want, you won't be disappointed. Almost every island claims the best in the region, and most people have their favorites. Some of the best known are Grenada's Grand Anse, Tobago's Pigeon Point, Martinique's Diamant beach, and Anguilla's Shoal Bay. The most popular beaches tend to be on the more sheltered west coasts; those on the Atlantic side are wilder, with strong currents and surf. Bathsheba, in Barbados, is the classic Atlantic beach, with giant boulders and formidable surf.

Only a handful of islands – Dominica, St. Vincent, Saba and Sint Eustatius – do not have extensive white beaches. This means that they have so far escaped the impact of mass tourism which has changed the landscape of places like Antigua. Their volcanoes, rivers, and dense rainforest make them ideal for environmental tourism, although locals point out that legions of "eco-tourists" can quickly spoil the pristine nature that they have come to see.

The region's variety, physical and cultural, makes some island-hopping essential to take in a mix of cultures. The best way to move along the island chain is with the locally-owned airline LIAT (unkindly assumed to stand for Leaving Island Any Time). Although notoriously unreliable, LIAT has a fleet of small planes which can take you to any of the region's airports. With a LIAT air pass it is feasible to visit several islands within two weeks. This involves a great deal of waiting around and a fair amount of bureaucracy but is certainly worth it.

From English-seeming Barbados it is a relief to reach Martinique or Guadeloupe, where food, fashions and plumbing bear the unmistakeable imprint of the *patrie*. Both French islands have a well-organized network of forest walks, and many of their historic sugar plantations and rum distilleries are open to the public. Both Fort-de-France and Pointe-à-Pitre have a scruffy Gallic charm and some interesting nineteenth-century architecture. The French islands' subsidized economies and high cost of living make them very expensive, and few locals speak English, but they offer another version of the Caribbean which should not be missed.

The Dutch islands offer no linguistic problems, since more people speak English than Dutch. Sint Maarten has its admirers, but many people find it an overcrowded, over-commercialized mess of condominiums and shopping malls. In complete contrast are Sint Eustatius and Saba, also part of the Dutch Kingdom. Sint Eustatius is a quiet, melancholy place, where derelict warehouses are the only reminder of a once-glorious past as a trading center. Saba, which until the 1950s had no airstrip and no road, is a picture-book island of white wooden houses and steep hillsides. Saba is developing a reputation as the best diving location in the Eastern Caribbean, so its ruritanian charm may not last much longer.

Among the English-speaking islands, Barbados and Antigua are the most tourism-dominated. Barbados is easy-going and perhaps rather unexciting, while Antigua's appeal is even less obvious. St. Kitts and Nevis specialize in up-market visitors, who stay in expensive restored plantation houses. Both islands are scenically spectacular, and Basseterre is one of the region's best preserved towns. Dominica is still largely undeveloped and welcoming, as is St. Vincent, but St. Lucia and Grenada are rapidly embracing large-scale tourism. All four islands have beautiful mountain landscapes and many natural attractions. Anguilla is the quietest island (there is nothing to do but sit on the beach) and Trinidad is the loudest and most culturally diverse. Not yet geared up for tourism, Trinidad has elements of Edwardian Britain (the Savannah), rural India (the Caroni district), and urban Africa. It is exciting and not normally restful.

There is, of course, a "high season" (mid-December to mid-April) and a "low season." You can expect to pay a lot more for everything in the high season, but will also avoid the risk of hurricanes which are most common from August until November. It is a good idea not to arrive in Trinidad during Carnival unless you want to go without sleep for three days.

Every island has at least one historical or natural sight which is worth a proper visit. Taxi-drivers will often be willing to act as guides (at a price) or it is always easy to hire a car (again, rarely cheap). The best-value and most adventurous way to reach out-of-town destinations is to take a minibus, most of which depart from a central location in the main town. Recommended visits in each island are as follows:

Anguilla: North of the Valley near Shoal Village is The Fountain national park, the centerpiece of which is a cave containing a fresh water spring and Arawak petroglyphs.

Antigua: English Harbour, an attractive yachting center on the island's south coast, contains Nelson's Dockyard, a complex of museums, craft shops, and art studios, which aim to illustrate aspects of life in eighteenth-century colonial Antigua. Above, Shirley Heights offer a superb view over English Harbour and surrounding countryside.

Barbados: There is a network of National Trust sites, most of which are certainly worth exploring. Andromeda Gardens near Bathsheba has an impressive array of tropical flora, while Codrington College is one of the best preserved examples of British colonial architecture in the Caribbean.

Dominica: Trafalgar Waterfalls are the island's most popular natural site, but there are often large cruise ship parties and aggressive local "guides." From Portsmouth on the northwest coast it is possible to visit ruined colonial forts and take a boat-trip up the spectacular Indian River.

Grenada: The Grand Etang National Park, about 7 miles inland from St. George's, is easily reached on the Grenville road. It contains a crater lake, ringed by thick rainforest, through which paths have been built. Several mountains can be climbed, the most scenic being Mount Qua Qua, but it is hard work.

Guadeloupe: Gosier on Grande-Terre is the tourist center of Guadeloupe and bustles with shops, bars, and restaurants. Quieter and architecturally better preserved than Pointe-à-Pitre is the former capital, Basse-Terre. On this mountainous wing of the island there are waterfalls, rainforest, and the still-active volcano of La Soufrière.

Martinique: There are plenty of well-marked hiking trails in the national parks. A trip to the former capital, Saint Pierre, reveals the extent of the 1902 volcano disaster; it is best to go from Fort-de-France along the Route de la Trace, a spectacular cross-island road which cuts through rainforest and mountain valleys. Also recommended is the beach at Diamant with its views of the famous Rocher du Diamant (Diamond Rock).

Montserrat: Galway's Plantation is a partly restored eighteenth-century sugar plantation with extensive views over sea and surrounding mountains. There are several pleasant walks in this small island, one of the best leading to the Great Alps Waterfall.

Saba: The quaint villages of The Bottom and Windwardside have much to offer with their pretty wooden houses and well-tended gardens. A steep, but manageable, walk up 1,064 steps takes you to the top of Mount Scenery and through some exotic forest landscapes.

St. Kitts: Brimstone Fortress, a dramatic and beautifully reconstructed monument to British military might, containing permanent exhibitions on the turbulent history of the fort. Several plantation houses, mostly now used as hotels, can be visited both in St. Kitts and Nevis, revealing some of the grandeur enjoyed by the slave-owning elites of yesteryear.

St. Lucia: The Pitons, the dramatic forest-covered peaks on the southwest coast, are among the region's most impressive sights. A visit here can be combined with a walk around Soufrière, a pretty and traditional town and a trip to the nearby Sulpher Springs, where bubbling mud and steam testify to the power of the volcanic geology.

St. Martin: Overcrowded and tourism-dominated, there are few points of interest beyond the veaches and shopping malls. The French side of the island is marginally less spoiled, and the village of Grand Case retains some Gallic charm.

St. Vincent: The Botanical Gardens in Kingstown are worth an expedition, containing a good variety of trees and plants, including Captain Bligh's breadfruit. The Leeward Highway which follows the west coast offers wonderful sea views as well as safe proximity to the Soufrière volcano. There are plenty of walks and waterfalls in one of the region's least built-up islands.

Sint Eustatius: The main attraction outside run-down Oranjestad is The Quill, a long extinct volcano, whose crater contains rainforest and a surprising variety of flora and fauna.

Trinidad & Tobago: Tobago's gentle landscape and idyllic beaches stand in contrast to the dramatic variety in Trinidad's countryside. Outside sprawling Port of Spain, you can visit bird sanctuaries, rainforest nature centers, and vast, deserted beaches lined by coconut plantations. The north coast, with Maracas Bay and the village of Blanchisseuse, is scenically stunning, while the famous Pitch Lake, an expanse of sticky asphalt, is certainly unusual if not beautiful.

TIPS FOR TRAVELERS

Safety

Apart from the smallest islands such as Anguilla and Saba, most places have their share of petty thieves and muggers. With the exception of certain poorer districts in the bigger cities like Port of Spain and Bridgetown, it is normally safe to walk anywhere during the day, but the usual care should be taken with jewelry, watches, and large sums of cash. Most hotels have a safety deposit box and it is always worth using it. At night there are definite no-go areas, especially deserted beaches, and caution should be exercised. Certain islands, especially St. Lucia, have more or less insistent hustlers who offer a range of services. Visitors should refuse firmly but always politely.

Health

There are no specific health risks attached to the Eastern Caribbean, and in general drinking water is safe. Standards of hygiene in street food stalls and the cheapest restaurants may not be too high, so it is worth avoiding stomach upsets by sticking to clean-looking establishments.

The most obvious problem is the danger of over-exposure to the sun, and extreme sunburn is common among foreign visitors. The hours of most intense sun are from midday to about 3 p.m., and sun creams should be used.

Doctors and hospitals are usually good, and most hotels will recommend a local doctor if problems occur.

Women Travelers

Women can expect some minor harassment in certain islands but also a good deal of consideration. Women tourists are now commonplace throughout the region and should not encounter particular problems if normal security precautions are taken.

Changing Money

All islands except the French overseas departments are more or less happy to accept U.S. dollars as well as local currency. The local currency is usually pegged to the dollar or pound at stable rates of exchange, and in some places local and foreign money are virtually interchangeble. Banks can be very slow and tend to close early, so it is worth ensuring that you have enough cash at any time, especially at weekends. It is not advisable to change money elsewhere, since hotels often offer a poor exchange rate. Credit cards are widely accepted.

Souvenirs

There are plenty of craft shops in each of the islands, and many hotels and airport stores offer the standard tourist fare of T-shirts and batik. You may prefer to try local markets for shopping, but these are not normally aimed at the souvenir-hunting visitor. Some island specialities are certainly worth taking home, not least rum, spices, and hot sauces. *Zouk* music is very popular in the region, but less known in Europe and the U.S., and CDs are widely available. Other artifacts include paintings and carvings of variable quality (often imported from Haiti), musical instruments and fabrics.

Children

Small children are very welcome in all areas of daily life, and travelers with children will probably make more contact with local people than those without. Children face no particular problems in the islands, but care should be taken regarding fast-moving traffic and sunburn.

Drugs

Ganja or marijuana is grown and widely available throughout the region. Other drugs such as cocaine and crack are increasingly used by a small minority, normally associated with the narcotics trade. It is advisable to refuse all offers of drugs, especially in islands such as Dominica where governments take a strong "moral" line on drugs and drug-smuggling.

FURTHER READING AND ADDRESSES

Beckles, H., *A History of Barbados: From Amerindian Settlement to Nation-State*, Cambridge, 1990.

Burton, R. and F. Reno (eds), *French and West Indian: Martinique, Guadeloupe and French Guiana Today*, Basingstoke, 1995.

Cameron, S. and B. Box, *The Caribbean Islands Handbook*, Bath, 1996. (annually updated)

Ellis, P. (ed), *Women of the Caribbean*, London, 1986.

Ferguson, J., *Grenada: Revolution in Reverse*, London, 1991.

Kincaid, J., *A Small Place*, London, 1988.

Lewis, G.K., *The Growth of the Modern West Indies*, New York, 1968.

McAfee, K., *Storm Signals: Structural Adjustment and Development Alternatives in the Caribbean*, London, 1991.

Pattullo, P., *Last Resorts: The Cost of Tourism in the Caribbean*, London, 1996.

Sutton, P. (ed), *Europe and the Caribbean*, Basingstoke, 1991.

Thomas, C.Y., *The Poor and the Powerless: Economic Policy and Change in the Caribbean*, London, 1988.

Williams, E., *From Columbus to Castro: The History of the Caribbean, 1492-1969*, London, 1970.

Wilson, M., *The Caribbean Environment*, Oxford, 1989.

Fiction and Poetry

Brathwaite, K., *Mother Poem*, Oxford, 1977.

Césaire, A., *Return to My Native Land*, London, 1969.

Condé, M., *Tree of Life*, London, 1994.

Lamming, G., *In the Castle of My Skin*, London, 1953.

Lovelace, E., *The Dragon Can't Dance*, London, 1979.

Rhys, J., *Wide Sargasso Sea*, London, 1966.

Schwarz-Bart, S., *Between Two Worlds*, Oxford, 1992.

Walcott, D., *Collected Poems*, London, 1993.

Local Bookstores

Anguilla: National Bookstore, The Valley

Barbados: Cloister Bookshop, Bridgetown

Dominica: Front Line, Queen Mary Street, Roseau

Grenada: Sea Change Book Shop, Carenage, St. George's

Guadeloupe: Librairie Générale, rue Schoelcher, Pointe-à-Pitre

St. Kitts: Walls Deluxe Records and Bookshop, Fort Street, Basseterre

St. Lucia: Sunshine Bookshop, Gablewoods Mall, Castries

St. Vincent: Noah's Arkade, Blue Caribbean Building, Kingstown

Trinidad: Metropolitan Books, Colsort Mall, Port of Spain

ADDRESSES AND CONTACTS

Travel Agents/Tour Operators
Transatlantic Wings/The Caribbean Experience,
70 Pembroke Road,
London W8 6NX, UK
Tel: 0171-602-4021
(Specialist travel agency and tour operator)

Last Frontiers,
Swan House, High Street,
Long Crendon, Bucks HP18 9AF, UK
Tel: 01844-208405
(Small group and individual tours to Dominica)

Alternative Travel Networks:
Tourism Concern,
Stapleton House,
277-281 Holloway Road,
London N7 8HN
Tel: 0171-753-3330

Center for Responsible Tourism,
PO Box 827,
San Anselmó,
CA 94979, U.S.A
(Research and advice on ethical tourism)

Global Exchange,
2017 Mission #303,
San Francisco, CA 94110, U.S.A
Tel: 415-255-7296
(Organizes fact-finding tours in the Caribbean)

Non-Governmental Organizations
Cooperation for Development,
118 Broad Street,
Chesham,
Buckinghamshire HP5 3ED, UK
Tel: 01494-775557
(Development agency with projects in the Eastern Caribbean)

Farmers Link,
38-40 Exchange Street,
Norwich NR2 1AX, UK
Tel: 01603 765670
(information on region's banana industry)

Caribbean Conservation Association,
Savannah Lodge, The Garrison,
St. Michael, Barbados
(Regional body, involved in heritage and environmental projects)

All of the English-speaking islands have high commissions and tourist offices in London and most in the U.S. and Canada. Enquiries concerning Martinique and Guadeloupe are dealt with by the French Tourist Office, 178 Piccadilly, London W1V 0AL (0891-244123).
In the U.S. contact Maison de la France, 444 Madison Avenue, New York, NY 10020-2452.

FACTS AND FIGURES

GEOGRAPHY

The islands which make up the Lesser Antilles (or Windward and Leeward islands) run down some 430 m. from Anguilla in the north to Grenada in the south. Trinidad & Tobago, although part of the Eastern Caribbean, are not counted as belonging to the Lesser Antilles, although Barbados, which lies to the east of the main island chain, is included.

Geology: The islands form a double arc, comprising an inner line from Saba to Grenada which is volcanic in origin, and a parallel outer line from Anguilla to Barbados which is made up of coral limestone built upon rock. The volcanic chain, which also includes Sint Eustatius, St. Kitts & Nevis, Montserrat, Guadeloupe (Basse-Terre), Dominica, Martinique, St. Lucia and St. Vincent, contains mostly inactive volcanoes, although those in Montserrat, Guadeloupe, Martinique and St. Vincent have erupted in the course of the twentieth century. Most volcanoes, known by the French word *soufrières*, produce steaming craters, hot water springs and pungent sulphur vents or "fumaroles". The terrain on the volcanic chain is mountainous, with peaks reaching about 5,000 ft. in islands such as Dominica, Guadeloupe and Martinique. The outer chain of coral limestone islands which comprises Anguilla, Antigua, Barbuda, Guadeloupe (Grande-Terre) and Barbados is characterized by flat terrain, formed by a wedge of sediments pushed up by the movement of tectonic plates. Trinidad & Tobago are of separate geological origin, having once been attached to the South American mainland in the ice ages when sea levels were lower. As a result, their flora and fauna are different from and richer than those of other islands.

Climate: The entire Eastern Caribbean lies in the tropical zone, with near-equable temperatures all year round. Daytime temperatures are normally between 77° and 86°F, dropping by 18°F at night. Rainfall is heavier between June and November, the period which includes the hurricane season. Average annual rainfall ranges from 36 inches (Anguilla) to 200 inches (Dominica).

Flora and Fauna: The region as a whole contains a number of distinctive geographical features. Coral reefs are still to be found off the coast of most islands, and some territories such as Saba and Tobago attract divers from around the world. Coastal wetlands, including mangroves, exist in Martinique, Dominica, and Trinidad, while primary rainforest is restricted to small areas in Guadeloupe. However, many islands have large areas of secondary forest, containing commercially valuable wood such as gommier, balata, and blue mahoe. On the flatter islands and in coastal regions, dry scrub woodland is more common, and many trees shed their leaves in the dry season. Flora and fauna very enormously between the islands. In flat, deforested, densely populated Barbados and St. Martin there are very few remote areas and few species; in islands such as Dominica and Martinique, where inaccessible terrain is still predominant, there is a profusion of plant and bird life. Several species (mongoose, agouti, opossum, and some monkeys) were introduced into the islands by man. The most common endemic species are birds, and several islands have distinct and protected birds such as the native parrots of St. Lucia and St. Vincent. Trinidad & Tobago have the richest range of bird life, with over 400 species recorded.

Infrastructure: varies from island to island according to terrain and economic development. Barbados and Trinidad have a developed network of good roads (900 m. and 5,000 m.), while islands such as St. Kitts or St. Vincent have a very limited transport network. There are no passenger train services in the region, and some islands have small railroad systems used in the sugar-cane industry. Most islands' main towns are also ports and, with the exception of Saba, every island has a functioning port. The most important are Port of Spain and Point Lisas (Trinidad), Fort-de-France (Martinique), and Pointe-à-Pitre (Guadeloupe). The largest international airports are those in Trinidad, Barbados, Grenada, Martinique, Guadeloupe, St. Martin and Antigua, all of which are capable of receiving wide-bodied jets. Other islands, especially St. Vincent and Dominica, have smaller airports, and tourists must change planes on other islands. Saba is reputed to have the shortest commercial runway in the world, measuring only 1,300 ft.

Education: Education in the English-speaking islands is free and, in theory, compulsory for an average of 11 years between the ages of 5 and 16. In Guadeloupe and Martinique education is free and compulsory between the ages of 6 and 16, as is the case in the Netherlands Antilles. There are branches of the University of the West Indies in Barbados and Trinidad and campuses of the Université Antilles-Guyane in Martinique and Guadeloupe.

Topography

Territory	Area (m2)	Highest Point (feet)	Position	Capital
Anguilla	35	213	18 13N 63 03W	The Valley
Antigua & Barbuda	170	1319	17 05N 61 48W	St. John's
Barbados	167	1115	13 10N 59 32W	Bridgetown
Dominica	290	4746	15 25N 61 20W	Roseau
Grenada	133	2755	20 07N 61 40W	St. George's
Montserrat	39	2998	16 45N 62 12W	Plymouth
St. Kitts & Nevis	104	3792	17 20N 62 45W	Basseterre
St. Lucia	238	3119	13 55N 61 00W	Castries
St. Vincent	150	4048	13 15N 61 11W	Kingstown
Trinidad & Tobago	1980	3083	10 30N 60 15W	Port of Spain
Guadeloupe	687	4868	16 16N 61 32W	Basse-Terre
Martinique	436	4582	14 40N 61 00W	Fort-de-France
Saba	5	2854	17 38N 63 14W	The Bottom
St. Eustatius	8	1968	17 29N 62 58W	Oranjestad
St. Maarten	13	1358	18 04W 63 04N	Philipsburg

POPULATION

Social Trends

Territory	Population (000's)	Population Growth (% 1990-95)	Population Density (people per m2)	Life Expectancy (years m/f)	Infant Mortality (per 1,000 live births)	Population per doctor
Anguilla	8.9	4.8	38			
Antigua & Barbuda	64.5	0.4	56	71/75	19.2	1,119
Barbados	263.5	0.4	236	73/78	10.1	1,042
Dominica	72.8	0.6	37	74/80	18.4	1,889
Grenada	95.5	0.5	107	68/72	12.7	1,617
Montserrat	10.6	-2.4	40			
St. Kitts & Nevis	42	(0.6)	60	63/69	20.0	972
St. Lucia	139.9	1.4	88	69/75	18.3	2,235
St. Vincent	108.4	1	108	71/74	19.0	2,690
Trinidad & Tobago	1246.9	0.9	94	68/73	17.0	1,275
Guadeloupe	387	1.7	84	70/77	10.4	680
Martinique	359.5	1	123	75/81	6.2	584
Saba	1.2	N/A	36	71/76	6.3	701
St. Eustatius	2.2	N/A	41	"	"	"
St. Maarten	35.5	N/A	403	"	"	"

Language and Religion

Territory	Illiteracy (%)	Languages(s)	Main Religion(s)
Anguilla	N/A	English	Anglican
Antigua & Barbuda	10%	English	Anglican
Barbados	2%	English	Anglican
Dominica	5.6%	English/Creole	Roman Catholic
Grenada	15%	English/Creole	Roman Catholic
Montserrat	N/A	English	Roman Catholic
St Kitts & Nevis	10%	English	Anglican
St Lucia	20%	English/Creole	Roman Catholic
St Vincent	15%	English	Anglican
Trinidad & Tobago	4.9%	English, Hindi, Urdu	Roman Catholic, Hindu, Muslim, Anglican
Guadeloupe	10%	French, Creole	Roman Catholic
Martinique	8%	French, Creole	Roman Catholic
Saba	5%	English, Dutch	Roman Catholic
St Eustatius	"	"	"
St Maarten	"	"	"

HISTORY AND POLITICS

Some key dates: * c. 4000-500 BC: Arawaks arrive from mainland South America * c. AD 1000-1500: Caribs supplant Arawaks in Eastern Caribbean * 1493: Christopher Columbus visits several islands on second expedition * 1623: rival British and French settlements established on St. Kitts * 1627: British colonize Barbados * 1635: French settle on Martinique * 1636: Dutch colonize St. Eustatius * 1648 French and Dutch agree to divide St. Martin * 1686: large-scale white convict labor sent from Britain to Barbados * 1747: discovery of sugar beet technology in Europe * 1763: Treaty of Paris; France retains Guadeloupe, Britain takes Canada * 1782: British fleet defeats French at Les Saintes * 1783: Treaty of Versailles; Britain wins back several colonies from France * 1794: revolutionary Convention in Paris abolishes slavery * 1795: Julien Fédon leads insurrection against British in Grenada * 1797: Spain relinquishes Trinidad to Britain * 1802: Napoleon Bonaparte restores slavery in Guadeloupe * 1807: Britain abolishes slave trade * 1817: France abolishes slave trade * 1833: Britain abolishes slavery * 1838: first inden-tured laborers from India arrive in Trinidad * 1848: France abolishes slavery * 1863: Holland abolishes slavery * 1902: eruption of Mont Pelée in Martinique kills 30,000; discovery of oil in Trinidad * 1934-8: social unrest in Trinidad, Barbados, St. Kitts, St. Lucia and St. Vincent * 1938-9: Moyne Commission investigates causes of unrest * 1946: Martinique and Guadeloupe vote to become French *départements* * 1954: proclamation of Charter of the Kingdom of the Netherlands * 1958-61: short-lived Federation of the West Indies * 1962: Trinidad & Tobago independent * 1966: Barbados independent * 1969: Britain "invades" Anguilla * 1970: "Black Power" revolt in Trinidad * 1974: Grenada independent * 1979: Grenada revolution ousts Eric Gairy * 1981: founding of Organization of Eastern Caribbean States: * 1983: murder of Maurice Bishop and U.S. invasion of Grenada * 1989: Hurricane Hugo devastates region * 1992: creation of European Union's Single European Market * 1995: Hurricane Luis hits several islands; Geest sells banana industry to Fyffes and island governments

Constitutions: The English-speaking islands are mostly constitutional monarchies within the Commonwealth, in which Queen Elizabeth II is nominally head of state. The exceptions are Trinidad & Tobago which became a republic within the Common-wealth in 1976 and Dominica which became an independent republic in 1978. Anguilla and Montserrat are British Dependent Territories, with representative government, a ministerial system, and the Queen as head of state. All are multi-party democracies with universal suffrage which hold regular elections. Martinique and Guadeloupe are *départements d'outre-mer* and integral parts of the French Republic. Each has a Prefect, appointed by the French Ministry of the Interior and elects a local legislature made up of a general council (which sits for six years) and a regional council which also includes the deputies and senators elected and sent to represent the islands in the French parliament. The head of state is the President of France. The Dutch territories of Saba, Sint Eustatius, and Sint Maarten belong to the Netherlands Antilles, itself a part of the Kingdom of the Netherlands. Each island has its own legislative and executive council and sends elected representatives to a federal parliament in Curaçao. The Queen of the Netherlands is the head of state.

Armed Forces: Antigua & Barbuda, Barbados, Dominica, Grenada, St. Kitts & Nevis, St. Lucia and St. Vincent are members of the Regional Security System (RSS), each contributing a small number of troops to the Barbados-based military unit. Trinidad & Tobago has an army of approximately 2,000 troops and a paramilitary police force numbering 4,800. A French military force of about 8,000 is maintained in Martinique, Guadeloupe, and French Guiana, while defense in the Netherlands Antilles is the responsibility of the Dutch government.

Membership of International Organizations: the English-speaking islands are members of the Caribbean Community (CARICOM) and seven English-speaking territories (Antigua & Barbuda, St. Kitts & Nevis, Montserrat, Dominica, Grenada, St. Lucia and St. Vincent) make up the Organization of Eastern Caribbean States (OECS). All English-speaking islands are also members of the Commonwealth. With the exception of the French DOMs and Dutch islands, the Eastern Caribbean islands belong to the UN and UN organizations and the Organization of American States (OAS). All CARICOM members are also members of the Association of Caribbean States, founded in 1994.

Media/communications: The bigger islands such as Barbados and Trinidad have choice of daily newspapers (*The Nation* in Barbados and *The Trinidad Guardian* are among the best-known); smaller islands usually have at least one weekly newspaper. *Caribbean Week*, published in Barbados, covers the whole of the region. Television and radio varies from island to island; Trinidad and the French islands have significant local output of television, while all territories have access to U.S. satellite and cable. All islands have local radio stations.

Political Status

Territory	Independence (former power)	Political Status	Main Political Party (June 1996)
Anguilla	UK	BDT (1)	Anguilla United Party
Antigua & Barbuda	1981 (UK)	Con. Monarchy (2)	Antigua Labour Party
Barbados	1966 (UK)	Con. Monarchy	Barbados Labour Party
Dominica	1978 (UK)	Republic	United Workers Party
Grenada	1974 (UK)	Con. Monarchy	New National Party
Montserrat	UK	BDT	National Progressive Party
St. Kitts & Nevis	1983 (UK)	Con. Monarchy	St. Kitts & Nevis Labour Party
St. Lucia	1979 (UK)	Con. Monarchy	United Workers Party
St. Vincent	1979 (UK)	Con. Monarchy	National Democratic Party
Trinidad &Tobago	1962 (UK)	Republic	United National Congress
Guadeloupe	France	département d'outre mer	N/A
Martinique	France	département d'outre mer	Parti Progressiste Martiniquais
Saba	Holland	Member Netherlands Antilles	Windward Islands People's Movement
St. Eustatius	Holland	Member Netherlands Antilles	Democratic Party
St. Maarten	Holland	Member Netherlands Antilles	St. Maarten Patriotic Alliance

(1) British Dependent Territory   (2) Constitutional Monarchy

ECONOMY

Territory	Currency	Per Capita GDP (US$ 1994)	Average GDP Growth (1990-95)	Inflation (1990-95)
Anguilla	EC$	6,153	5.5%	4.0%
Antigua & Barbuda	EC$	7,702	1.7%	2.2%
Barbados	B$	6,578	0.5%	0.6%
Dominica	EC$	2,825	1.2%	3.3%
Grenada	EC$	2,810	2.5%	3.0%
Montserrat	EC$	5,846	(8.3%)	4.7%
St. Kitts & Nevis	EC$	4,889	3.5%	2.9%
St. Lucia	EC$	3,596	3.6%	3.3%
St. Vincent	EC$	2,390	3.3%	2.3%
Trinidad & Tobago	TT$	3,847	1.6%	7.0%
Guadeloupe	FF	6,970	N/A	2.3%
Martinique	FF	8,250	N/A	3.8%
Saba	NA Florin	8,320	N/A	3.0%
St. Eustatius	"	"	"	"
St. Maarten	"	"	"	"

Territory	Imports (US$m 1994)	Exports (US$m 1994)	Tourism Earnings (US$m 1994)	External Debt (US$m 1994)
Anguilla	62.7	63.2	51.0	14.0
Antigua & Barbuda	433.0	440.8	394.0	240.2
Barbados	866.6	1,003.4	597.6	442.0
Dominica	131.7	95.6	30.6	102.3
Grenada	168.0	127.7	59.3	79.3
Montserrat	44.3	30.1	18.5	10.3
St. Kitts & Nevis	143.8	120.2	76.2	45.3
St. Lucia	369.5	336.9	224.1	105.2
St. Vincent	157.7	93.7	50.5	81.1
Trinidad & Tobago	1,247.6	2,011.8	77.3	2,052.5
Guadeloupe	1,509.0	130	269.0	N/A
Martinique	1,750.0	247	282.0	N/A
Saba	N/A	N/A	N/A	N/A
St. Eustatius	"	"	"	"
St. Maarten	"	"	"	"